THE GLENCOE LITERATURE LIBRARY

Our Town

with Related Readings

 Glencoe
McGraw-Hill

New York, New York   Columbus, Ohio   Woodland Hills, California   Peoria, Illinois

Acknowledgments

Grateful acknowledgment is given authors, publishers, photographers, museums, and agents for permission to reprint the following copyrighted material. Every effort has been made to determine copyright owners. In case of any omissions, the Publisher will be pleased to make suitable acknowledgments in future editions.

Excerpts from *White Lilacs*, copyright © 1993 by Carolyn Meyer, reprinted by permission of Harcourt, Inc.

"Because I could not stop for Death" reprinted by permission of the publishers and the Trustees of Amherst College from *The Poems of Emily Dickinson*, Thomas H. Johnson, ed., Cambridge, Mass.: The Belknap Press of Harvard University Press, Copyright © 1951, 1955, 1979 by the President and Fellows of Harvard College.

Excerpt from *Main Street: The Story of Carol Kennicott* by Sinclair Lewis, copyright 1920 by Harcourt, Inc. and renewed 1948 by Sinclair Lewis, reprinted by permission of the publisher.

"Theater Review: *Our Town*" by Brooks Atkinson. *New York Times*, February 5, 1938. Copyright © 1938 by the New York Times Co. Reprinted by permission.

"Prologue for *The Comstock Journals* (or *Sotol City Blues*)" by Olivia G. Castellanos. Reprinted by permission of the author.

Caution: Professionals and amateurs are hereby warned that *Our Town*, being fully protected under the copyright laws of the United States of America, the United Kingdom, Canada, and all other countries of the Copyright Union, is subject to a royalty. All rights, including, but not limited to, professional, amateur, motion picture, recitation, lecturing, public reading, radio broadcasting, television, video or sound taping, all other forms of mechanical or electronic reproduction, such as information storage and retrieval systems and photocopying, and the rights of translation into foreign languages are strictly reserved. All inquiries concerning all rights (other than amateur) should be addressed to the author's agent, Robert A. Freedman Dramatic Agency, Inc., 1501 Broadway, Suite 2310, New York, NY, 10036, without whose permission in writing no performance of the play must be made. All inquiries concerning the amateur acting rights should be addressed to Samuel French, Inc., 45 West 25th Street, New York, NY 10010. No amateur performance of the play may be given without obtaining in advance the written permission of Samuel French, Inc., and paying the requisite royalty fee.

Acknowledgments continued on page 98.

Glencoe/McGraw-Hill

A Division of The McGraw·Hill Companies

Send all inquiries to:
Glencoe/McGraw-Hill
8787 Orion Place
Columbus, OH 43240

ISBN 0-07-828408-2
Printed in the United States of America
2 3 4 5 6 7 8 9 026 04 03 02

Contents

Our Town

Thornton Wilder

CHARACTERS (in the order of their appearance)

STAGE MANAGER

DR. GIBBS

JOE CROWELL

HOWIE NEWSOME

MRS. GIBBS

MRS. WEBB

GEORGE GIBBS

REBECCA GIBBS

WALLY WEBB

EMILY WEBB

PROFESSOR WILLARD

MR. WEBB

PROFESSOR WILLARD

MR. WEBB

WOMAN IN THE BALCONY

MAN IN THE AUDITORIUM

LADY IN THE BOX

SIMON STIMSON

MRS. SOAMES

CONSTABLE WARREN

SI CROWELL

THREE BASEBALL PLAYERS

SAM CRAIG

JOE STODDARD

The entire play takes place in Grover's Corners,
New Hampshire.

Act I

No curtain.

    No scenery.

    The audience, arriving, sees an empty stage in half-light.

    Presently the STAGE MANAGER, *hat on and pipe in mouth, enters and begins placing a table and three chairs downstage left, and a table and three chairs downstage right.*

    He also places a low bench at the corner of what will be the Webb house, left.

    "Left" and "right" are from the point of view of the actor facing the audience. "Up" is toward the back wall.

    As the house lights go down he has finished setting the stage and leaning against the right proscenium pillar watches the late arrivals in the audience.

    When the auditorium is in complete darkness he speaks:

STAGE MANAGER.   This play is called "Our Town." It was written by Thornton Wilder; produced and directed by A. . . .(or: produced by A. . . .; directed by B. . . .). In it you will see Miss C. . . .; Miss D. . . .; Miss E. . . .; and Mr. F. . . .; Mr. G. . . .; Mr. H. . . .; and many others. The name of the town is Grover's Corners, New Hampshire—just across the Massachusetts line: latitude 42 degrees 40 minutes; longitude 70 degrees 37 minutes. The First Act shows a day in our town. The day is May 7, 1901. The time is just before dawn.

    A rooster crows.

The sky is beginning to show some streaks of light over in the East there, behind our mount'in.

The morning star always gets wonderful bright the minute before it has to go,—doesn't it?

    He stares at it for a moment, then goes upstage.

Well, I'd better show you how our town lies. Up here—

    That is: parallel with the back wall.

is Main Street. Way back there is the railway station; tracks go that way. Polish Town's across the tracks, and some Canuck families.

Toward the left.

Over there is the Congregational Church; across the street's the Presbyterian.

Methodist and Unitarian are over there.

Baptist is down on the holla' by the river.

Catholic Church is over beyond the tracks.

Here's the Town Hall and Post Office combined; jail's in the basement.

Bryan once made a speech from these very steps here.

Along here's a row of stores. Hitching posts and horse blocks in front of them. First automobile's going to come along in about five years—belonged to Banker Cartwright, our richest citizen . . . lives in the big white house up on the hill.

Here's the grocery store and here's Mr. Morgan's drugstore. Most everybody in town manages to look into those two stores once a day.

Public School's over yonder. High School's still farther over. Quarter of nine mornings, noontimes, and three o'clock afternoons, the hull town can hear the yelling and screaming from those schoolyards.

He approaches the table and chairs downstage right.

This is our doctor's house,—Doc Gibbs'. This is the back door.

Two arched trellises, covered with vines and flowers, are pushed out, one by each proscenium pillar.

There's some scenery for those who think they have to have scenery.

This is Mrs. Gibbs' garden. Corn . . . peas . . . beans . . . hollyhocks . . . heliotrope . . . and a lot of burdock.

Crosses the stage.

In those days our newspaper come out twice a week—the Grover's Corners *Sentinel*—and this is Editor Webb's house.

And this is Mrs. Webb's garden.

Just like Mrs. Gibbs', only it's got a lot of sunflowers, too.

He looks upward, center stage.

Right here . . . 's a big butternut tree.

He returns to his place by the right proscenium pillar and looks at the audience for a minute.

Nice town, y'know what I mean?

Nobody very remarkable ever come out of it, s'far as we know.

The earliest tombstones in the cemetery up there on the mountain say 1670–1680—they're Grovers and Cartwrights and Gibbses and Herseys— same names as are around here now.

Well, as I said: it's about dawn.

The only lights on in town are in a cottage over by the tracks where a Polish mother's just had twins. And in the Joe Crowell house, where Joe Junior's getting up so as to deliver the paper. And in the depot, where Shorty Hawkins is gettin' ready to flag the 5:45 for Boston.

A train whistle is heard. The STAGE MANAGER *takes out his watch and nods.*

Naturally, out in the country—all around—there've been lights on for some time, what with milkin's and so on. But town people sleep late.

So—another day's begun.

There's Doc Gibbs comin' down Main Street now, comin' back from that baby case. And here's his wife comin' downstairs to get breakfast.

MRS. GIBBS, *a plump, pleasant woman in the middle thirties, comes "downstairs" right. She pulls up an imaginary window shade in her kitchen and starts to make a fire in her stove.*

Doc Gibbs died in 1930. The new hospital's named after him.

Mrs. Gibbs died first—long time ago, in fact. She went out to visit her daughter, Rebecca, who married an insurance man in Canton, Ohio, and died there—pneumonia—but her body was brought back here. She's up in the cemetery there now—in with a whole mess of Gibbses and Herseys— she was Julia Hersey 'fore she married Doc Gibbs in the Congregational Church over there.

In our town we like to know the facts about everybody.

There's Mrs. Webb, coming downstairs to get her breakfast, too.

—That's Doc Gibbs. Got that call at half past one this morning.

And there comes Joe Crowell, Jr., delivering Mr. Webb's *Sentinel*.

DR. GIBBS *has been coming along Main Street from the left. At the point where he would turn to approach his house, he stops, sets down his—imaginary— black bag, takes off his hat, and rubs his face with fatigue, using an enormous handkerchief.*

MRS. WEBB, *a thin, serious, crisp woman, has entered her kitchen, left, tying on an apron. She goes through the motions of putting wood into a stove, lighting it, and preparing breakfast.*

Suddenly, JOE CROWELL, JR., *eleven, starts down Main Street from the right, hurling imaginary newspapers into doorways.*

JOE CROWELL, JR. Morning, Doc Gibbs.

DR. GIBBS. Morning, Joe.

JOE CROWELL, JR. Somebody been sick, Doc?

DR. GIBBS. No. Just some twins born over in Polish Town.

JOE CROWELL, JR. Do you want your paper now?

DR. GIBBS. Yes, I'll take it.—Anything serious goin' on in the world since Wednesday?

JOE CROWELL, JR. Yessir. My schoolteacher, Miss Foster, 's getting married to a fella over in Concord.

DR. GIBBS. I declare.—How do you boys feel about that?

JOE CROWELL, JR. Well, of course, it's none of my business—but I think if a person starts out to be a teacher she ought to stay one.

DR. GIBBS. How's your knee, Joe?

JOE CROWELL, JR. Fine, Doc, I never think about it at all. Only like you said, it always tells me when it's going to rain.

DR. GIBBS. What's it telling you today? Goin' to rain?

JOE CROWELL, JR. No, sir.

DR. GIBBS. Sure?

JOE CROWELL, JR. Yessir.

DR. GIBBS. Knee ever make a mistake?

JOE CROWELL, JR. No, sir.

JOE *goes off.* DR. GIBBS *stands reading his paper.*

STAGE MANAGER. Want to tell you something about that boy Joe Crowell there. Joe was awful bright—graduated from high school here, head of his class. So he got a scholarship to Massachusetts Tech. Graduated head of his class there, too. It was all wrote up in the Boston paper at the time. Goin' to be a great engineer, Joe was. But the war broke out and he died in France. —All that education for nothing.

HOWIE NEWSOME.

Off left.

Giddap, Bessie! What's the matter with you today?

STAGE MANAGER. Here comes Howie Newsome, deliverin' the milk.

HOWIE NEWSOME, about thirty, in overalls, comes along Main Street from the left, walking beside an invisible horse and wagon and carrying an imaginary rack with milk bottles. The sound of clinking milk bottles is heard. He leaves some bottles at Mrs. Webb's trellis, then, crossing the stage to Mrs. Gibbs', he stops center to talk to Dr. Gibbs.

HOWIE NEWSOME. Morning, Doc.

DR. GIBBS. Morning, Howie.

HOWIE NEWSOME. Somebody sick?

DR. GIBBS. Pair of twins over to Mrs. Goruslawski's.

HOWIE NEWSOME. Twins, eh? This town's gettin' bigger every year.

DR. GIBBS. Goin' to rain, Howie?

HOWIE NEWSOME. No, no. Fine day—that'll burn through. Come on, Bessie.

DR. GIBBS. Hello Bessie.

He strokes the horse, which has remained up center.

How old is she, Howie?

HOWIE NEWSOME. Going on seventeen. Bessie's all mixed up about the route ever since the Lockharts stopped takin' their quart of milk every day. She wants to leave 'em a quart just the same—keeps scolding me the hull trip.

He reaches Mrs. Gibbs' back door. She is waiting for him.

MRS. GIBBS. Good morning, Howie.

HOWIE NEWSOME.   Morning, Mrs. Gibbs. Doc's just comin' down the street.

MRS. GIBBS.   Is he? Seems like you're late today.

HOWIE NEWSOME.   Yes. Somep'n went wrong with the separator. Don't know what 'twas.

He passes Dr. Gibbs up center.

Doc!

DR. GIBBS.   Howie!

MRS. GIBBS.

Calling upstairs.

Children! Children! Time to get up.

HOWIE NEWSOME.   Come on, Bessie!

He goes off right.

MRS. GIBBS.   George! Rebecca!

DR. GIBBS *arrives at his back door and passes through the trellis into his house.*

MRS. GIBBS.   Everything all right, Frank?

DR. GIBBS.   Yes. I declare—easy as kittens.

MRS. GIBBS.   Bacon'll be ready in a minute. Set down and drink your coffee. You can catch a couple hours' sleep this morning, can't you?

DR. GIBBS.   Hm! . . . Mrs. Wentworth's coming at eleven. Guess I know what it's about, too. Her stummick ain't what it ought to be.

MRS. GIBBS.   All told, you won't get more'n three hours' sleep. Frank Gibbs, I don't know what's goin' to become of you. I do wish I could get you to go away someplace and take a rest. I think it would do you good.

MRS. WEBB.   Emileeee! Time to get up! Wally! Seven o'clock!

MRS. GIBBS.   I declare, you got to speak to George. Seems like something's come over him lately. He's no help to me at all. I can't even get him to cut me some wood.

DR. GIBBS.

Washing and drying his hands at the sink. MRS. GIBBS *is busy at the stove.*

Is he sassy to you?

MRS. GIBBS. No. He just whines! All he thinks about is that baseball— George! Rebecca! You'll be late for school.

DR. GIBBS. M-m-m . . .

MRS. GIBBS. George!

DR. GIBBS. George, look sharp!

GEORGE'S VOICE. Yes, Pa!

DR. GIBBS.

As he goes off the stage.

Don't you hear your mother calling you? I guess I'll go upstairs and get forty winks.

MRS. WEBB. Walleee! Emileee! You'll be late for school! Walleee! You wash yourself good or I'll come up and do it myself.

REBECCA GIBBS' VOICE. Ma! What dress shall I wear?

MRS. GIBBS. Don't make a noise. Your father's been out all night and needs his sleep. I washed and ironed the blue gingham for you special.

REBECCA. Ma, I hate that dress.

MRS. GIBBS. Oh, hush-up-with-you.

REBECCA. Every day I go to school dressed like a sick turkey.

MRS. GIBBS. Now, Rebecca, you always look *very* nice.

REBECCA. Mama, George's throwing soap at me.

MRS. GIBBS. I'll come and slap the both of you,—that's what I'll do.

A factory whistle sounds.

The CHILDREN dash in and take their places at the tables. Right, GEORGE, about sixteen, and REBECCA, eleven. Left, EMILY and WALLY, same ages. They carry strapped schoolbooks.

STAGE MANAGER. We've got a factory in our town too—hear it? Makes blankets. Cartwrights own it and it brung 'em a fortune.

MRS. WEBB. Children! Now I won't have it. Breakfast is just as good as any other meal and I won't have you gobbling like wolves. It'll stunt your growth,—that's a fact. Put away your book, Wally.

WALLY. Aw, ma! By ten o'clock I got to know all about Canada.

MRS. WEBB. You know the rule's well as I do—no books at table. As for me, I'd rather have my children healthy than bright.

EMILY. I'm both, Mama: you know I am. I'm the brightest girl in school for my age. I have a wonderful memory.

MRS. WEBB. Eat your breakfast.

WALLY. I'm bright, too, when I'm looking at my stamp collection.

MRS. GIBBS. I'll speak to your father about it when he's rested. Seems to me twenty-five cents a week's enough for a boy your age. I declare I don't know how you spend it all.

GEORGE. Aw, Ma,—I gotta lotta things to buy.

MRS. GIBBS. Strawberry phosphates—that's what you spend it on.

GEORGE. I don't see how Rebecca comes to have so much money. She has more'n a dollar.

REBECCA.

Spoon in mouth, dreamily.

I've been saving it up gradual.

MRS. GIBBS. Well, dear, I think it's a good thing to spend some money every now and then.

REBECCA. Mama, do you know what I love most in the world—do you?— Money.

MRS. GIBBS. Eat your breakfast.

THE CHILDREN. Mama, there's first bell.—I gotta hurry.—I don't want any more.—I gotta hurry.

The CHILDREN rise, seize their books and dash out through the trellises. They meet, down center, and chattering, walk to Main Street, then turn left.

The STAGE MANAGER goes off, unobtrusively, right.

MRS. WEBB. Walk fast, but you don't have to run. Wally, pull up your pants at the knee. Stand up straight, Emily.

MRS. GIBBS. Tell Miss Foster I send her my best congratulations—can you remember that?

REBECCA. Yes, Ma.

MRS. GIBBS. You look real nice, Rebecca. Pick up your feet.

ALL. Good-by.

MRS. GIBBS fills her apron with food for the chickens and comes down to the footlights.

MRS. GIBBS. Here, chick, chick, chick.

No, go away, you. Go away.

Here, chick, chick, chick.

What's the matter with *you*? Fight, fight, fight,—that's all you do.

Hm . . . *you* don't belong to me. Where'd you come from?

She shakes her apron.

Oh, don't be so scared. Nobody's going to hurt you.

MRS. WEBB is sitting on the bench by her trellis, stringing beans.

Good morning, Myrtle. How's your cold?

MRS. WEBB. Well, I still get that tickling feeling in my throat. I told Charles I didn't know as I'd go to choir practice tonight. Wouldn't be any use.

MRS. GIBBS. Have you tried singing over your voice?

MRS. WEBB. Yes, but somehow I can't do that and stay on the key. While I'm resting myself I thought I'd string some of these beans.

MRS. GIBBS.

Rolling up her sleeves as she crosses the stage for a chat.

Let me help you. Beans have been good this year.

MRS. WEBB. I've decided to put up forty quarts if it kills me. The children say they hate 'em, but I notice they're able to get 'em down all winter.

Pause. Brief sound of chickens cackling.

MRS. GIBBS. Now, Myrtle. I've got to tell you something, because if I don't tell somebody, I'll burst.

MRS. WEBB. Why, Julia Gibbs!

MRS. GIBBS. Here, give me some more of those beans. Myrtle, did one of those secondhand-furniture men from Boston come to see you last Friday?

MRS. WEBB. No-o.

MRS. GIBBS.   Well, he called on me. First I thought he was a patient wantin' to see Dr. Gibbs. 'N he wormed his way into my parlor, and, Myrtle Webb, he offered me three hundred and fifty dollars for Grandmother Wentworth's highboy, as I'm sitting here!

MRS. WEBB.   Why, Julia Gibbs!

MRS. GIBBS.   He did! That old thing! Why, it was so big I didn't know where to put it and I almost give it to Cousin Hester Wilcox.

MRS. WEBB.   Well, you're going to take it, aren't you?

MRS. GIBBS.   I don't know.

MRS. WEBB.   You don't know—three hundred and fifty dollars! What's come over you?

MRS. GIBBS.   Well, if I could get the Doctor to take the money and go away someplace on a real trip, I'd sell it like that.—Y'know, Myrtle, it's been the dream of my life to see Paris, France.—Oh, I don't know. It sounds crazy, I suppose, but for years I've been promising myself that if we ever had the chance—

MRS. WEBB.   How does the Doctor feel about it?

MRS. GIBBS.   Well, I did beat about the bush a little and said that if I got a legacy—that's the way I put it—I'd make him take me somewhere.

MRS. WEBB.   M-m-m . . . What did he say?

MRS. GIBBS.   You know how he is. I haven't heard a serious word out of him since I've known him. No, he said, it might make him discontented with Grover's Corners to go traipsin' about Europe; better let well enough alone, he says. Every two years he makes a trip to the battlefields of the Civil War and that's enough treat for anybody, he says.

MRS. WEBB.   Well, Mr. Webb just *admires* the way Dr. Gibbs knows everything about the Civil War. Mr. Webb's a good mind to give up Napoleon and move over to the Civil War, only Dr. Gibbs being one of the greatest experts in the country just makes him despair.

MRS. GIBBS.   It's a fact! Dr. Gibbs is never so happy as when he's at Antietam or Gettysburg. The times I've walked over those hills, Myrtle, stopping at every bush and pacing it all out, like we were going to buy it.

MRS. WEBB.   Well, if that secondhand man's really serious about buyin' it, Julia, you sell it. And then you'll get to see Paris, all right. Just keep droppin' hints from time to time—that's how I got to see the Atlantic Ocean, y'know.

MRS. GIBBS. Oh, I'm sorry I mentioned it. Only it seems to me that once in your life before you die you ought to see a country where they don't talk in English and don't even want to.

The STAGE MANAGER *enters briskly from the right. He tips his hat to the ladies, who nod their heads.*

STAGE MANAGER. Thank you, ladies. Thank you very much.

MRS. GIBBS *and* MRS. WEBB *gather up their things, return into their homes and disappear.*

Now we're going to skip a few hours.

But first we want a little more information about the town, kind of a scientific account, you might say.

So I've asked Professor Willard of our State University to sketch in a few details of our past history here.

Is Professor Willard here?

PROFESSOR WILLARD, *a rural savant, pince-nez on a wide satin ribbon, enters from the right with some notes in his hand.*

May I introduce Professor Willard of our State University.

A few brief notes, thank you, Professor,—unfortunately our time is limited.

PROFESSOR WILLARD. Grover's Corners . . . let me see . . . Grover's Corners lies on the old Pleistocene granite of the Appalachian range. I may say it's some of the oldest land in the world. We're very proud of that. A shelf of Devonian basalt crosses it with vestiges of Mesozoic shale, and some sandstone outcroppings; but that's all more recent: two hundred, three hundred million years old.

Some highly interesting fossils have been found . . . I may say: unique fossils . . . two miles out of town, in Silas Peckham's cow pasture. They can be seen at the museum in our University at any time—that is, at any reasonable time. Shall I read some of Professor Gruber's notes on the meteorological situation—mean precipitation, et cetera?

STAGE MANAGER. Afraid we won't have time for that, Professor. We might have a few words on the history of man here.

PROFESSOR WILLARD.   Yes . . . anthropological data: Early Amerindian stock. Cotahatchee tribes . . . no evidence before the tenth century of this era . . . hm . . . now entirely disappeared . . . possible traces in three families. Migration toward the end of the seventeenth century of English brachio-cephalic blue-eyed stock . . . for the most part. Since then some Slav and Mediterranean—

STAGE MANAGER.   And the population, Professor Willard?

PROFESSOR WILLARD.   Within the town limits: 2,640.

STAGE MANAGER.   Just a moment, Professor.

He whispers into the professor's ear.

PROFESSOR WILLARD.   Oh, yes, indeed?—The population, *at the moment,* is 2,642. The Postal District brings in 507 more, making a total of 3,149.—Mortality and birth rates: constant.—By MacPherson's gauge: 6.032.

STAGE MANAGER.   Thank you very much Professor. We're all very much obliged to you, I'm sure.

PROFESSOR WILLARD.   Not at all, sir; not at all.

STAGE MANAGER.   This way, Professor, and thank you again.

Exit PROFESSOR WILLARD.

Now the political and social report: Editor Webb.—Oh, Mr. Webb?

MRS. WEBB *appears at her back door.*

MRS. WEBB.   He'll be here in a minute . . . He just cut his hand while he was eatin' an apple.

STAGE MANAGER.   Thank you, Mrs. Webb.

MRS. WEBB.   Charles! Everybody's waitin'.

Exit MRS. WEBB.

STAGE MANAGER.   Mr. Webb is Publisher and Editor of the Grover's Corners *Sentinel.* That's our local paper, y'know.

MR. WEBB *enters from his house, pulling on his coat. His finger is bound in a handkerchief.*

MR. WEBB.   Well . . . I don't have to tell you that we're run here by a Board of Selectmen.—All males vote at the age of twenty-one. Woman vote indirect. We're lower middle class: sprinkling of professional men . . . ten per cent illiterate laborers. Politically, we're eighty-six per cent Republicans; six per cent Democrats; four per cent Socialists; rest, indifferent.

Religiously, we're eighty-five percent Protestants; twelve per cent Catholics; rest, indifferent.

STAGE MANAGER. Have you any comments, Mr. Webb?

MR. WEBB. Very ordinary town, if you ask me. Little better behaved than most. Probably a lot duller.

But our young people here seem to like it well enough. Ninety percent of 'em graduating from high school settle down right here to live—even when they've been away to college.

STAGE MANAGER. Now, is there anyone in the audience who would like to ask Editor Webb anything about the town?

WOMAN IN THE BALCONY. Is there much drinking in Grover's Corners?

MR. WEBB. Well, ma'am, I wouldn't know what you'd call *much*. Satiddy nights the farmhands meet down in Ellery Greenough's stable and holler some. We've got one or two town drunks, but they're always having remorses every time an evangelist comes to town. No, ma'am, I'd say likker ain't a regular thing in the home here, except in the medicine chest. Right good for snake bite, y'know—always was.

BELLIGERENT MAN AT THE BACK OF AUDITORIUM. Is there no one in town aware of—

STAGE MANAGER. Come forward, will you, where we can all hear you— What were you saying?

BELLIGERENT MAN. Is there no one in town aware of social injustice and industrial inequality?

MR. WEBB. Oh, yes, everybody is—somethin' terrible. Seems like they spend most of their time talking about who's rich and who's poor.

BELLIGERENT MAN. Then why don't they do something about it?

He withdraws without waiting for an answer.

MR. WEBB. Well, I dunno. . . . I guess we're all hunting like everybody else for a way the diligent and sensible can rise to the top and the lazy and quarrelsome can sink to the bottom. But it ain't easy to find. Meanwhile, we do all we can to help those that can't help themselves and those that can we leave alone.—Are there any other questions?

LADY IN A BOX. Oh, Mr. Webb? Mr. Webb, is there any culture or love of beauty in Grover's Corners?

MR. WEBB. Well, ma'am, there ain't much—not in the sense you mean. Come to think of it, there's some girls that play the piano at High School Commencement; but they ain't happy about it. No, ma'am, there isn't much culture; but maybe this is the place to tell you that we've got a lot of pleasures of a kind here: we like the sun comin' up over the mountain in the morning, and we all notice a good deal about the birds. We pay a lot of attention to them. And we watch the change of the seasons; yes, everybody knows about them. But those other things—you're right, ma'am,—there ain't much.—*Robinson Crusoe* and the Bible; and Handel's "Largo," we all know that; and Whistler's "Mother"—those are just about as far as we go.

LADY IN A BOX. So I thought. Thank you, Mr. Webb.

STAGE MANAGER. Thank you, Mr. Webb.

MR. WEBB *retires*.

Now, we'll go back to the town. It's early afternoon. All 2,642 have had their dinners and all the dishes have been washed.

MR. WEBB, *having removed his coat, returns and starts pushing a lawn mower to and fro beside his house.*

There's an early-afternoon calm in our town: a buzzin' and a hummin' from the school buildings; only a few buggies on Main Street—the horses dozing at the hitching posts; you all remember what it's like. Doc Gibbs is in his office, tapping people and making them say "ah." Mr. Webb's cuttin' his lawn over there; one man in ten thinks it's a privilege to push his own lawn mower.

No, sir. It's later than I thought. There are the children coming home from school already.

Shrill girls' voices are heard, off left. EMILY *comes along Main Street, carrying some books. There are some signs that she is imagining herself to be a lady of startling elegance.*

EMILY. I can't, Lois. I've got to go home and help my mother. I *promised.*

MR. WEBB. Emily, walk simply. Who do you think you are today?

EMILY. Papa, you're terrible. One minute you tell me to stand up straight and the next minute you call me names. I just don't listen to you.

She gives him an abrupt kiss.

MR. WEBB. Golly, I never got a kiss from such a great lady before.

He goes out of sight. EMILY *leans over and picks some flowers by the gate of her house.*

GEORGE GIBBS *comes careening down Main Street. He is throwing a ball up to dizzying heights, and waiting to catch it again. This sometimes requires his taking six steps backward. He bumps into an* OLD LADY *invisible to us.*

GEORGE. Excuse me, Mrs. Forrest.

STAGE MANAGER.

As Mrs. Forrest.

Go out and play in the fields, young man. You got no business playing baseball on Main Street.

GEORGE. Awfully sorry, Mrs. Forrest.—Hello, Emily.

EMILY. H'lo.

GEORGE. You made a fine speech in class.

EMILY. Well . . . I was really ready to make a speech about the Monroe Doctrine, but at the last minute Miss Corcoran made me talk about the Louisiana Purchase instead. I worked an awful long time on both of them.

GEORGE. Gee, it's funny, Emily. From my window up there I can just see your head nights when you're doing your homework over in your room.

EMILY. Why, can you?

GEORGE. You certainly do stick to it, Emily. I don't see how you can sit still that long. I guess you like school.

EMILY. Well, I always feel it's something you have to go through.

GEORGE. Yeah.

EMILY. I don't mind it really. It passes the time.

GEORGE. Yeah.—Emily, what do you think? We might work out a kinda telegraph from your window to mine; and once in a while you could give me a kinda hint or two about one of those algebra problems. I don't mean the answers, Emily of course not . . . just some little hint . . .

EMILY. Oh, I think *hints* are allowed.—So—ah—if you get stuck, George, you whistle to me; and I'll give you some hints.

GEORGE. Emily, you're just naturally bright, I guess.

EMILY. I figure that it's just the way a person's born.

GEORGE. Yeah. But, you see, I want to be a farmer, and my Uncle Luke says whenever I'm ready I can come over and work on his farm and if I'm any good I can just gradually have it.

EMILY. You mean the house and everything?

Enter MRS. WEBB *with a large bowl and sits on the bench by her trellis.*

GEORGE. Yeah. Well, thanks . . . I better be getting out to the baseball field. Thanks for the talk, Emily.—Good afternoon, Mrs. Webb.

MRS. WEBB. Good afternoon, George.

GEORGE. So long, Emily.

EMILY. So long, George.

MRS. WEBB. Emily, come and help me string these beans for the winter. George Gibbs let himself have a real conversation, didn't he? Why, he's growing up. How old would George be?

EMILY. I don't know.

MRS. WEBB. Let's see. He must be almost sixteen.

EMILY. Mama, I made a speech in class today and I was very good.

MRS. WEBB. You must recite it to your father at supper. What was it about?

EMILY. The Louisiana Purchase. It was like silk off a spool. I'm going to make speeches all my life.—Mama, are these big enough?

MRS. WEBB. Try and get them a little bigger if you can.

EMILY. Mama, will you answer me a question, serious?

MRS. WEBB. Seriously, dear—not serious.

EMILY. Seriously,—will you?

MRS. WEBB. Of course, I will.

EMILY. Mama, am I good looking?

MRS. WEBB. Yes, of course you are. All my children have got good features; I'd be ashamed if they hadn't.

EMILY. Oh, Mama, that's not what I mean. What I mean is: am I *pretty*?

MRS. WEBB. I've already told you, yes. Now that's enough of that. You have a nice young pretty face. I never heard of such foolishness.

EMILY.   Oh, Mama, you never tell us the truth about anything.

MRS. WEBB.   I *am* telling you the truth.

EMILY.   Mama, were *you* pretty?

MRS. WEBB.   Yes, I was, if I do say it. I was the prettiest girl in town next to Mamie Cartwright.

EMILY.   But, Mama, you've got to say *some*thing about me. Am I pretty enough . . . to get anybody . . . to get people interested in me?

MRS. WEBB.   Emily, you make me tired. Now stop it. You're pretty enough for all normal purposes.—Come along now and bring that bowl with you.

EMILY.   Oh, Mama, you're no help at all.

STAGE MANAGER.   Thank you. Thank you! That'll do. We'll have to interrupt again here. Thank you, Mrs. Webb; thank you, Emily.

> MRS. WEBB *and* EMILY *withdraw.*

There are some more things we want to explore about this town.

> *He comes to the center of the stage. During the following speech the lights gradually dim to darkness, leaving only a spot on him.*

I think this is a good time to tell you that the Cartwright interests have just begun building a new bank in Grover's Corners—had to go to Vermont for the marble, sorry to say. And they've asked a friend of mine what they should put in the cornerstone for people to dig up . . . a thousand years from now . . . Of course, they've put in a copy of the *New York Times* and a copy of Mr. Webb's *Sentinel*. . . . We're kind of interested in this because some scientific fellas have found a way of painting all that reading matter with a glue—a silicate glue—that'll make it keep a thousand—two thousand years.

We're putting in a Bible . . . and the Constitution of the United States— and a copy of William Shakespeare's plays. What do you say, folks? What do you think?

Y'know—Babylon once had two million people in it, and all we know about 'em is the names of the kings and some copies of wheat contracts . . . and contracts for the sale of slaves. Yet every night all those families sat down to supper, and the father came home from his work, and the smoke went up the chimney,—same as here. And even in Greece and Rome, all we know about the *real* life of the people is what we can piece together out of the joking poems and the comedies they wrote for the theatre back then.

So I'm going to have a copy of this play put in the cornerstone and the people a thousand years from now'll know a few simple facts about us— more than the Treaty of Versailles and the Lindbergh flight.

See what I mean?

So—people a thousand years from now—this is the way we were in the provinces north of New York at the beginning of the twentieth century.— This is the way we were: in our growing up and in our marrying and in our living and in our dying.

> *A choir partially concealed in the orchestra pit has begun singing "Blessed Be the Tie That Binds."*
>
> SIMON STIMSON *stands directing them.*
>
> *Two ladders have been pushed onto the stage; they serve as indication of the second story in the Gibbs and Webb houses.* GEORGE *and* EMILY *mount them, and apply themselves to their schoolwork.*
>
> DR. GIBBS *has entered and is seated in his kitchen reading.*

Well!—good deal of time's gone by. It's evening.

You can hear choir practice going on in the Congregational Church.

The children are at home doing their schoolwork.

The day's running down like a tired clock.

SIMON STIMSON. Now look here, everybody. Music come into the world to give pleasure.—Softer! Softer! Get it out of your heads that music's only good when it's loud. You leave loudness to the Methodists. You couldn't beat 'em, even if you wanted to. Now again. Tenors!

GEORGE. Hssst! Emily!

EMILY. Hello.

GEORGE. Hello!

EMILY. I can't work at all. The moonlight's so *terrible.*

GEORGE. Emily, did you get the third problem?

EMILY. Which?

GEORGE. The *third?*

EMILY. Why, yes, George—that's the easiest of them all.

GEORGE. I don't see it. Emily, can you give me a hint?

EMILY. I'll tell you one thing: the answer's in yards.

GEORGE. !!! In yards? How do you mean?

EMILY. In *square* yards.

GEORGE. Oh . . . in square yards.

EMILY. Yes, George, don't you see?

GEORGE. Yeah.

EMILY. In square yards of *wallpaper*.

GEORGE. Wallpaper,—oh, I see. Thanks a lot, Emily.

EMILY. You're welcome. My, isn't the moonlight *terrible*? And choir practice going on.—I think if you hold your breath you can hear the train all the way to Contoocook. Hear it?

GEORGE. M-m-m—What do you know!

EMILY. Well, I guess I better go back and try to work.

GEORGE. Good night, Emily. And thanks.

EMILY. Good night, George.

SIMON STIMSON. Before I forget it: how many of you will be able to come in Tuesday afternoon and sing at Fred Hersey's wedding?—show your hands. That'll be fine; that'll be right nice. We'll do the same music we did for Jane Trowbridge's last month.

—Now we'll do: "Art Thou Weary; Art Thou Languid?" It's a question, ladies and gentlemen, make it talk. Ready.

DR. GIBBS. Oh, George, can you come down a minute?

GEORGE. Yes, Pa.

He descends the ladder.

DR. GIBBS. Make yourself comfortable, George; I'll only keep you a minute. George, how old are you?

GEORGE. I? I'm sixteen, almost seventeen.

DR. GIBBS. What do you want to do after school's over?

GEORGE. Why, you know, Pa. I want to be a farmer on Uncle Luke's farm.

DR. GIBBS. You'll be willing, will you, to get up early and milk and feed the stock . . . and you'll be able to hoe and hay all day?

GEORGE. Sure, I will. What are you . . . what do you mean, Pa?

DR. GIBBS. Well, George, while I was in my office today I heard a funny sound . . . and what do you think it was? It was your mother chopping wood. There you see your mother—getting up early; cooking meals all day long; washing and ironing;—and still she has to go out in the back yard and chop wood. I suppose she just got tired of asking you. She just gave up and decided it was easier to do it herself. And you eat her meals, and put on the clothes she keeps nice for you, and you run off and play baseball,—like she's some hired girl we keep around the house but that we don't like very much. Well, I knew all I had to do was call your attention to it. Here's a handkerchief, son. George, I've decided to raise your spending money twenty-five cents a week. Not, of course, for chopping wood for your mother, because that's a present you give her, but because you're getting older—and I imagine there are lots of things you must find to do with it.

GEORGE. Thanks, Pa.

DR. GIBBS. Let's see—tomorrow's your payday. You can count on it—Hmm. Probably Rebecca'll feel she ought to have some more too. Wonder what could have happened to your mother. Choir practice never was as late as this before.

GEORGE. It's only half past eight, Pa.

DR. GIBBS. I don't know why she's in that old choir. She hasn't any more voice than an old crow. . . . Traipsin' around the streets at this hour of the night . . . Just about time you retired, don't you think?

GEORGE. Yes, Pa.

GEORGE *mounts to his place on the ladder.*

Laughter and good nights can be heard on stage left and presently MRS. GIBBS, MRS. SOAMES *and* MRS. WEBB *come down Main Street. When they arrive at the corner of the stage they stop.*

MRS. SOAMES. Good night, Martha. Good night, Mr. Foster.

MRS. WEBB. I'll tell Mr. Webb; I *know* he'll want to put it in the paper.

MRS. GIBBS. My, it's late!

MRS. SOAMES. Good night, Irma.

MRS. GIBBS. Real nice choir practice, wa'n't it? Myrtle Webb! Look at that moon, will you! Tsk-tsk-tsk. Potato weather, for sure.

They are silent a moment, gazing up at the moon.

MRS. SOAMES. Naturally I didn't want to say a word about it in front of those others, but now we're alone—really, it's the worst scandal that ever was in town!

MRS. GIBBS. What?

MRS. SOAMES. Simon Stimson!

MRS. GIBBS. Now, Louella!

MRS. SOAMES. But, Julia! To have the organist of a church *drink* and *drunk* year after year. You know he was drunk tonight.

MRS. GIBBS. Now, Louella! We all know about Mr. Stimson, and we all know about the troubles he's been through, and Dr. Ferguson knows too, and if Dr. Ferguson keeps him on there in his job the only thing the rest of us can do is just not to notice it.

MRS. SOAMES. *Not to notice it!* But it's getting worse.

MRS. WEBB. No, it isn't, Louella. It's getting better. I've been in that choir twice as long as you have. It doesn't happen anywhere near so often. . . . My, I hate to go to bed on a night like this.—I better hurry. Those children'll be sitting up till all hours. Good night, Louella.

They all exchange good nights. She hurries downstage, enters her house and disappears.

MRS. GIBBS. Can you get home safe, Louella?

MRS. SOAMES. It's as bright as day. I can see Mr. Soames scowling at the window now. You'd think we'd been to a dance the way the men-folk carry on.

More good nights. MRS. GIBBS *arrives at her home and passes through the trellis into the kitchen.*

MRS. GIBBS. Well, we had a real good time.

DR. GIBBS. You're late enough.

MRS. GIBBS. Why, Frank, it ain't any later 'n usual.

DR. GIBBS. And you stopping at the corner to gossip with a lot of hens.

MRS. GIBBS. Now, Frank, don't be grouchy. Come out and smell the heliotrope in the moonlight.

They stroll out arm in arm along the footlights.

Isn't that wonderful? What did you do all the time I was away?

DR. GIBBS. Oh, I read—as usual. What were the girls gossiping about tonight?

MRS. GIBBS. Well, believe me, Frank—there is something to gossip about.

DR. GIBBS. Hmm! Simon Stimson far gone, was he?

MRS. GIBBS. Worst I've ever seen him. How'll that end, Frank? Dr. Ferguson can't forgive him forever.

DR. GIBBS. I guess I know more about Simon Stimson's affairs than anybody in this town. Some people ain't made for small-town life. I don't know how that'll end; but there's nothing we can do but just leave it alone. Come, get in.

MRS. GIBBS. No, not yet . . . Frank, I'm worried about you.

DR. GIBBS. What are you worried about?

MRS. GIBBS. I think it's my duty to make plans for you to get a real rest and change. And if I get that legacy, well, I'm going to insist on it.

DR. GIBBS. Now, Julia, there's no sense in going over that again.

MRS. GIBBS. Frank, you're just *unreasonable!*

DR. GIBBS.

Starting into the house.

Come on, Julia, it's getting late. First thing you know you'll catch cold. I gave George a piece of my mind tonight. I reckon you'll have your wood chopped for a while anyway. No, no, start getting upstairs.

MRS. GIBBS. Oh, dear. There's always so many things to pick up, seems like. You know, Frank, Mrs. Fairchild always locks her front door every night. All those people up that part of town do.

DR. GIBBS.

Blowing out the lamp.

They're all getting citified, that's the trouble with them. They haven't got nothing fit to burgle and everybody knows it.

They disappear.

REBECCA *climbs up the ladder beside* GEORGE.

GEORGE. Get out, Rebecca. There's only room for one at this window. You're always spoiling everything.

REBECCA. Well, let me look just a minute.

GEORGE. Use your own window.

REBECCA. I did, but there's no moon there. . . . George, do you know what I think, do you? I think maybe the moon's getting nearer and nearer and there'll be a big 'splosion.

GEORGE. Rebecca, you don't know anything. If the moon were getting nearer, the guys that sit up all night with telescopes would see it first and they'd tell about it, and it'd be in all the newspapers.

REBECCA. George, is the moon shining on South America, Canada and half the whole world?

GEORGE. Well—prob'ly is.

The STAGE MANAGER *strolls on.*

Pause. The sound of crickets is heard.

STAGE MANAGER. Nine thirty. Most of the lights are out. No, there's Constable Warren trying a few doors on Main Street. And here comes Editor Webb, after putting his newspaper to bed.

MR. WARREN, *an elderly policeman, comes along Main Street from the right,* MR. WEBB *from the left.*

MR. WEBB. Good evening, Bill.

CONSTABLE WARREN. Evenin', Mr. Webb.

MR. WEBB. Quite a moon!

CONSTABLE WARREN. Yepp.

MR. WEBB. All quiet tonight?

CONSTABLE WARREN. Simon Stimson is rollin' around a little. Just saw his wife movin' out to hunt for him so I looked the other way—there he is now.

SIMON STIMSON *comes down Main Street from the left, only a trace of unsteadiness in his walk.*

MR. WEBB. Good evening, Simon . . . Town seems to have settled down for the night pretty well. . . .

SIMON STIMSON *comes up to him and pauses a moment and stares at him, swaying slightly.*

Good evening . . . Yes, most of the town's settled down for the night, Simon. . . . I guess we better do the same. Can I walk along a ways with you?

> SIMON STIMSON *continues on his way without a word and disappears at the right.*

Good night.

CONSTABLE WARREN. I don't know how that's goin' to end, Mr. Webb.

MR. WEBB. Well, he's seen a peck of trouble, one thing after another. . . . Oh, Bill, if you see my boy smoking cigarettes, just give him a word, will you? He thinks a lot of you, Bill.

CONSTABLE WARREN. I don't think he smokes no cigarettes, Mr. Webb. Leastways, not more'n two or three a year.

MR. WEBB. Hm . . . I hope not.—Well, good night, Bill.

CONSTABLE WARREN. Good night, Mr. Webb.

> *Exit.*

MR. WEBB. Who's that up there? Is that you, Myrtle?

EMILY. No, it's me, Papa.

MR. WEBB. Why aren't you in bed?

EMILY. I don't know. I just can't sleep yet, Papa. The moonlight's so *won-derful*. And the smell of Mrs. Gibbs' heliotrope. Can you smell it?

MR. WEBB. Hm . . . Yes. Haven't any troubles on your mind, have you Emily?

EMILY. *Troubles*, Papa? *No.*

MR. WEBB. Well, enjoy yourself, but don't let your mother catch you. Good night, Emily.

EMILY. Good night, Papa.

> MR. WEBB *crosses into the house, whistling "Blessed Be the Tie That Binds" and disappears.*

REBECCA. I never told you about that letter Jane Crofut got from her minister when she was sick. He wrote Jane a letter and on the envelope the address was like this: It said: Jane Crofut; The Crofut Farm; Grover's Corners; Sutton County; New Hampshire; United States of America.

GEORGE. What's funny about that?

REBECCA. But listen, it's not finished: the United States of America; Continent of North America; Western Hemisphere; the Earth; the Solar System; the Universe; the Mind of God—that's what it said on the envelope.

GEORGE. What do you know!

REBECCA. And the postman brought it just the same.

GEORGE. What do you know!

STAGE MANAGER. That's the end of the First Act, friends. You can go and smoke now, those that smoke.

Act II

The tables and chairs of the two kitchens are still on the stage.
The ladders and the small bench have been withdrawn.
The STAGE MANAGER *has been at his accustomed place watching the audience return to its seats.*

STAGE MANAGER.   Three years have gone by.

Yes, the sun's come up over a thousand times.

Summers and winters have cracked the mountains a little bit more and the rains have brought down some of the dirt.

Some babies that weren't even born before have begun talking regular sentences already; and a number of people who thought they were right young and spry have noticed that they can't bound up a flight of stairs like they used to, without their heart fluttering a little.

All that can happen in a thousand days.

Nature's been pushing and contriving in other ways, too: a number of young people fell in love and got married.

Yes, the mountain got bit away a few fractions of an inch; millions of gallons of water went by the mill; and here and there a new home was set up under a roof.

Almost everybody in the world gets married,—you know what I mean? In our town there aren't hardly any exceptions. Most everybody in the world climbs into their graves married.

The First Act was called the Daily Life. This act is called Love and Marriage. There's another act coming after this: I reckon you can guess what that's about.

So:

It's three years later. It's 1904.

It's July 7th, just after High School Commencement.

That's the time most of our young people jump up and get married.

Soon as they've passed their last examinations in solid geometry and Cicero's Orations, looks like they suddenly feel themselves fit to be married.

It's early morning. Only this time it's been raining. It's been pouring and thundering.

Mrs. Gibbs' garden, and Mrs. Webb's here: drenched.

All those bean poles and pea vines: drenched.

All yesterday over there on Main Street, the rain looked like curtains being blown along.

Hm . . . it may begin again any minute.

There! You can hear the 5:45 for Boston.

> MRS. GIBBS *and* MRS. WEBB *enter their kitchen and start the day as in the First Act.*

And there's Mrs. Gibbs and Mrs. Webb come down to make breakfast, just as though it were an ordinary day. I don't have to point out to the women in my audience that those ladies they see before them, both of those ladies cooked three meals a day—one of 'em for twenty years, the other for forty—and no summer vacation. They brought up two children apiece, washed, cleaned the house,—and *never a nervous breakdown.*

It's like what one of those Middle West poets said: You've got to love life to have life, and you've got to have life to love life. . . . It's what they call a vicious circle.

HOWIE NEWSOME.

> *Off stage left.*

Giddap, Bessie!

STAGE MANAGER. Here comes Howie Newsome delivering the milk. And there's Si Crowell delivering the papers like his brother before him.

> SI CROWELL *has entered hurling imaginary newspapers into doorways;* HOWIE NEWSOME *has come along Main Street with Bessie.*

SI CROWELL. Morning, Howie.

HOWIE NEWSOME. Morning, Si.—Anything in the papers I ought to know?

SI CROWELL. Nothing much, except we're losing about the best baseball pitcher Grover's Corners ever had—George Gibbs.

HOWIE NEWSOME. Reckon he is.

SI CROWELL. He could hit and run bases, too.

HOWIE NEWSOME. Yep. Mighty fine ball player.—Whoa! Bessie! I guess I can stop and talk if I've a mind to!

SI CROWELL. I don't see how he could give up a thing like that just to get married. Would you, Howie?

HOWIE NEWSOME. Can't tell, Si. Never had no talent that way.

CONSTABLE WARREN *enters. They exchange good mornings.*

You're up early, Bill.

CONSTABLE WARREN. Seein' if there's anything I can do to prevent a flood. River's been risin' all night.

HOWIE NEWSOME. Si Crowell's all worked up here about George Gibbs' retiring from baseball.

CONSTABLE WARREN. Yes, sir; that's the way it goes. Back in '84 we had a player, Si—even George Gibbs couldn't touch him. Name of Hank Todd. Went down to Maine and become a parson. Wonderful ball player.— Howie, how does the weather look to you?

HOWIE NEWSOME. Oh, 'tain't bad. Think maybe it'll clear up for good.

CONSTABLE WARREN *and* SI CROWELL *continue on their way.*

HOWIE NEWSOME *brings the milk first to Mrs. Gibbs' house. She meets him by the trellis.*

MRS. GIBBS. Good morning, Howie. Do you think it's going to rain again?

HOWIE NEWSOME. Morning, Mrs. Gibbs. It rained so heavy, I think maybe it'll clear up.

MRS. GIBBS. Certainly hope it will.

HOWIE NEWSOME. How much did you want today?

MRS. GIBBS. I'm going to have a houseful of relations, Howie. Looks to me like I'll need three-a-milk and two-a-cream.

HOWIE NEWSOME. My wife says to tell you we both hope they'll be very happy, Mrs. Gibbs. Know they *will*.

MRS. GIBBS. Thanks a lot, Howie. Tell your wife I hope she gits there to the wedding.

HOWIE NEWSOME. Yes, she'll be there; she'll be there if she kin.

HOWIE NEWSOME *crosses to Mrs. Webb's house.*

Morning, Mrs. Webb.

MRS. WEBB. Oh, good morning, Mr. Newsome. I told you four quarts of milk, but I hope you can spare me another.

HOWIE NEWSOME. Yes'm . . . and the two of cream.

MRS. WEBB. Will it start raining again, Mr. Newsome?

HOWIE NEWSOME. Well. Just sayin' to Mrs. Gibbs as how it may lighten up. Mrs. Newsome told me to tell you how we hope they'll both be very happy, Mrs. Webb. Know they *will.*

MRS. WEBB. Thank you, and thank Mrs. Newsome and we're counting on seeing you at the wedding.

HOWIE NEWSOME. Yes, Mrs. Webb. We hope to git there. Couldn't miss that. Come on, Bessie.

Exit HOWIE NEWSOME.

DR. GIBBS *descends in shirt sleeves, and sits down at his breakfast table.*

DR. GIBBS. Well, Ma, the day has come. You're losin' one of your chicks.

MRS. GIBBS. Frank Gibbs, don't you say another word. I feel like crying every minute. Sit down and drink your coffee.

DR. GIBBS. The groom's up shaving himself—only there ain't an awful lot to shave. Whistling and singing, like he's glad to leave us.—Every now and then he says "I do" to the mirror, but it don't sound convincing to me.

MRS. GIBBS. I declare, Frank, I don't know how he'll get along. I've arranged his clothes and seen to it he's put warm things on,—Frank! they're too *young.* Emily won't think of such things. He'll catch his death of cold within a week.

DR. GIBBS. I was remembering my wedding morning, Julia.

MRS. GIBBS. Now, don't start that, Frank Gibbs.

DR. GIBBS. I was the scaredest young fella in the State of New Hampshire. I thought I'd make a mistake for sure. And when I saw you comin' down the aisle I thought you were the prettiest girl I'd ever seen, but the only trouble was that I'd never seen you before. There I was in the Congregational Church marryin' a total stranger.

MRS. GIBBS. And how do you think I felt!—Frank, weddings are perfectly awful things. Farces,—that's what they are!

She puts a plate before him.

Here, I've made something for you.

DR. GIBBS. Why, Julia Hersey—French toast!

MRS. GIBBS. 'Tain't hard to make and I had to do *something.*

Pause. DR. GIBBS *pours on the syrup.*

DR. GIBBS. How'd you sleep last night, Julia?

MRS. GIBBS. Well, I heard a lot of the hours struck off.

DR. GIBBS. Ye-e-s! I get a shock every time I think of George setting out to be a family man—that great gangling thing!—I tell you Julia, there's nothing so terrifying in the world as a *son.* The relation of father and son is the darndest, awkwardest—

MRS. GIBBS. Well, mother and daughter's no picnic, let me tell you.

DR. GIBBS. They'll have a lot of troubles, I suppose, but that's none of our business. Everybody has a right to their own troubles.

MRS. GIBBS.

At the table, drinking her coffee, meditatively.

Yes . . . people are meant to go through life two by two. 'Tain't natural to be lonesome.

Pause. DR. GIBBS *starts laughing.*

DR. GIBBS. Julia, do you know one of the things I was scared of when I married you?

MRS. GIBBS. Oh, go along with you!

DR. GIBBS. I was afraid we wouldn't have material for conversation more'n'd last us a few weeks.

Both laugh.

I was afraid we'd run out and eat our meals in silence, that's a fact.—Well, you and I been conversing for twenty years now without any noticeable barren spells.

MRS. GIBBS. Well,—good weather, bad weather—'tain't very choice, but I always find something to say.

She goes to the foot of the stairs.

Did you hear Rebecca stirring around upstairs?

DR. GIBBS. No. Only day of the year Rebecca hasn't been managing everybody's business up there. She's hiding in her room.—I got the impression she's crying.

MRS. GIBBS. Lord's sakes!—This has got to stop.—Rebecca! Rebecca! Come and get your breakfast.

GEORGE *comes rattling down the stairs, very brisk.*

GEORGE. Good morning, everybody. Only five more hours to live.

Makes the gesture of cutting his throat, and a loud "k-k-k," and starts through the trellis.

MRS. GIBBS. George Gibbs, where are you going?

GEORGE. Just stepping across the grass to see my girl.

MRS. GIBBS. Now, George! You put on your overshoes. It's raining torrents. You don't go out of this house without you're prepared for it.

GEORGE. Aw, Ma. It's just a *step!*

MRS. GIBBS. George! You'll catch your death of cold and cough all through the service.

DR. GIBBS. George, do as your mother tells you!

DR. GIBBS *goes upstairs.*

GEORGE *returns reluctantly to the kitchen and pantomimes putting on overshoes.*

MRS. GIBBS. From tomorrow on you can kill yourself in all weathers, but while you're in my house you'll live wisely, thank you.—Maybe Mrs. Webb isn't used to callers at seven in the morning.—Here, take a cup of coffee first.

GEORGE. Be back in a minute.

He crosses the stage, leaping over the puddles.

Good morning, Mother Webb.

MRS. WEBB. Goodness! You frightened me!—Now, George, you can come in a minute out of the wet, but you know I can't ask you in.

GEORGE. Why not—?

MRS. WEBB. George, you know 's well as I do: the groom can't see his bride on his wedding day, not until he sees her in church.

GEORGE. Aw!—that's just a superstition.—Good morning, Mr. Webb.

Enter MR. WEBB.

MR. WEBB. Good morning, George.

GEORGE. Mr. Webb, you don't believe in that superstition, do you?

MR. WEBB. There's a lot of common sense in some superstitions, George.

He sits at the table, facing right.

MRS. WEBB. Millions have folla'd it, George, and you don't want to be the first to fly in the face of custom.

GEORGE. How is Emily?

MRS. WEBB. She hasn't waked up yet. I haven't heard a sound out of her.

GEORGE. Emily's *asleep!!!*

MRS. WEBB. No wonder! We were up 'til all hours, sewing and packing. Now I'll tell you what I'll do; you set down here a minute with Mr. Webb and drink this cup of coffee; and I'll go upstairs and see she doesn't come down and surprise you. There's some bacon, too; but don't be long about it.

Exit MRS. WEBB.

Embarrassed silence.

MR. WEBB *dunks doughnuts in his coffee.*

More silence.

MR. WEBB.

Suddenly and loudly.

Well, George, how are you?

GEORGE.

Startled, choking over his coffee.

Oh, fine, I'm fine.

Pause.

Mr. Webb, what sense could there be in a superstition like that?

MR. WEBB.   Well, you see,—on her wedding morning a girl's head's apt to be full of . . . clothes and one thing and another. Don't you think that's probably it?

GEORGE.   Ye-e-s. I never thought of that.

MR. WEBB.   A girl's apt to be a mite nervous on her wedding day.

Pause.

GEORGE.   I wish a fellow could get married without all that marching up and down.

MR. WEBB.   Every man that's ever lived has felt that way about it, George; but it hasn't been any use. It's the womenfolk who've built up weddings, my boy. For a while now the women have it all their own. A man looks pretty small at a wedding, George. All those good women standing shoulder to shoulder making sure that the knot's tied in a mighty public way.

GEORGE.   But . . . you *believe* in it, don't you, Mr. Webb?

MR. WEBB.

With alacrity.

Oh, yes; *oh, yes.* Don't you misunderstand me, my boy. Marriage is a wonderful thing,—wonderful thing. And don't you forget that, George.

GEORGE.   No, sir.—Mr. Webb, how old were you when you got married?

MR. WEBB.   Well, you see: I'd been to college and I'd taken a little time to get settled. But Mrs. Webb—she wasn't much older than what Emily is. Oh, age hasn't much to do with it, George,—not compared with . . . uh . . . other things.

GEORGE.   What were you going to say, Mr. Webb?

MR. WEBB.   Oh, I don't know.—Was I going to say something?

Pause.

George, I was thinking the other night of some advice my father gave me when I got married. Charles, he said, Charles, start out early showing who's boss, he said. Best thing to do is to give an order, even if it don't make sense; just so she'll learn to obey. And he said: if anything about your wife irritates you—her conversation, or anything—just get up and leave the house. That'll make it clear to her, he said. And, oh, yes! he said never, *never* let your wife know how much money you have, never.

GEORGE.   Well, Mr. Webb . . . I don't think I could . . .

MR. WEBB. So I took the opposite of my father's advice and I've been happy ever since. And let that be a lesson to you, George, never to ask advice on personal matters.—George, are you going to raise chickens on your farm?

GEORGE. What?

MR. WEBB. Are you going to raise chickens on your farm?

GEORGE. Uncle Luke's never been much interested, but I thought—

MR. WEBB. A book came into my office the other day, George, on the Philo System of raising chickens. I want you to read it. I'm thinking of beginning in a small way in the back yard, and I'm going to put an incubator in the cellar—

Enter MRS. WEBB.

MRS. WEBB. Charles, are you talking about that old incubator again? I thought you two'd be talking about things worth while.

MR. WEBB.

Bitingly.

Well, Myrtle, if you want to give the boy some good advice, I'll go upstairs and leave you alone with him.

MRS. WEBB.

Pulling GEORGE *up.*

George, Emily's got to come downstairs and eat her breakfast. She sends you her love but she doesn't want to lay eyes on you. Good-by.

GEORGE. Good-by.

GEORGE *crosses the stage to his own home, bewildered and crestfallen. He slowly dodges a puddle and disappears into his house.*

MR. WEBB. Myrtle, I guess you don't know about that older superstition.

MRS. WEBB. What do you mean, Charles?

MR. WEBB. Since the cave men: no bridegroom should see his father-in-law on the day of the wedding, or near it. Now remember that.

Both leave the stage.

STAGE MANAGER. Thank you very much, Mr. and Mrs. Webb.—Now I have to interrupt again here. You see, we want to know how all this began—

this wedding, this plan to spend a lifetime together. I'm awfully interested in how big things like that begin.

You know how it is: you're twenty-one or twenty-two and you make some decisions; then whisssh! you're seventy: you've been a lawyer for fifty years, and that white-haired lady at your side has eaten over fifty thousand meals with you.

How do such things begin?

George and Emily are going to show you now the conversation they had when they first knew that . . . that . . . as the saying goes . . . they were meant for one another.

But before they do it I want you to try and remember what it was like to have been very young.

And particularly the days when you were first in love; when you were like a person sleepwalking, and you didn't quite see the street you were in, and didn't quite hear everything that was said to you.

You're just a little bit crazy. Will you remember that, please?

Now they'll be coming out of high school at three o'clock. George has just been elected President of the Junior Class, and as it's June, that means he'll be president of the Senior Class all next year. And Emily's just been elected Secretary and Treasurer.

I don't have to tell you how important that is.

> *He places a board across the backs of two chairs, which he takes from those at the Gibbs family's table. He brings two high stools from the wings and places them behind the board. Persons sitting on the stools will be facing the audience. This is the counter of Mr. Morgan's drugstore. The sounds of young people's voices are heard off left.*

Yepp,—there they are coming down Main Street now.

> EMILY, *carrying an armful of—imaginary—schoolbooks, comes along Main Street from the left.*

EMILY. I can't, Louise. I've got to go home. Good-by. Oh, Ernestine! Ernestine! Can you come over tonight and do Latin? Isn't that Cicero the worst thing—! Tell your mother you *have* to. G'by. G'by, Helen. G'by, Fred.

> GEORGE, *also carrying books, catches up with her.*

GEORGE. Can I carry your books home for you, Emily?

EMILY.

Coolly.

Why . . . uh . . . Thank you. It isn't far.

She gives them to him.

GEORGE. Excuse me a minute, Emily.—Say, Bob, if I'm a little late, start practice anyway. And give Herb some long high ones.

EMILY. Good-by, Lizzy.

GEORGE. Good-By, Lizzy.—I'm awfully glad you were elected, too, Emily.

EMILY. Thank you.

They have been standing on Main Street, almost against the back wall. They take the first steps toward the audience when GEORGE *stops and says:*

GEORGE. Emily, why are you mad at me?

EMILY. I'm not mad at you.

GEORGE. You've been treating me so funny lately.

EMILY. Well, since you ask me, I might as well say it right out, George,—

She catches sight of a teacher passing.

Good-by, Miss Corcoran.

GEORGE. Good-by, Miss Corcoran.—Wha—what is it?

EMILY.

Not scoldingly; finding it difficult to say.

I don't like the whole change that's come over you in the last year. I'm sorry if that hurts your feelings, but I've got to—tell the truth and shame the devil.

GEORGE. A *change?*—Wha—what do you mean?

EMILY. Well, up to a year ago I used to like you a lot. And I used to watch you as you did everything . . . because we'd been friends so long . . . and then you began spending all your time at *baseball* . . . and you never stopped to speak to anybody any more. Not even to your own family you didn't . . . and, George, it's a fact, you've got awful conceited and stuck-up, and all the girls say so. They may not say so to your face, but that's what they say about you behind your back, and it hurts me to hear them say it, but I've got to agree with them a little. I'm sorry if it hurts your feelings . . . but I can't be sorry I said it.

GEORGE.   I . . . I'm glad you said it, Emily. I never thought that such a thing was happening to me. I guess it's hard for a fella not to have faults creep into his character.

They take a step or two in silence, then stand still in misery.

EMILY.   I always expect a man to be perfect and I think he should be.

GEORGE.   Oh . . . I don't think it's possible to be perfect, Emily.

EMILY.   Well, my *father* is, and as far as I can see *your* father is. There's no reason on earth why you shouldn't be too.

GEORGE.   Well, I feel it's the other way round. That men aren't naturally good; but girls are.

EMILY.   Well, you might as well know right now that I'm not perfect. It's not as easy for a girl to be perfect as a man, because we girls are more—more—nervous.—Now I'm sorry I said all that about you. I don't know what made me say it.

GEORGE.   Emily,—

EMILY.   Now I can see it's not the truth at all. And I suddenly feel that it isn't important, anyway.

GEORGE.   Emily . . . would you like an ice-cream soda, or something, before you go home?

EMILY.   Well, thank you . . . I would.

They advance toward the audience and make an abrupt right turn, opening the door of Morgan's drugstore. Under strong emotion, EMILY *keeps her face down.* GEORGE *speaks to some passers-by.*

GEORGE.   Hello, Stew,—how are you?—Good afternoon, Mrs. Slocum.

The STAGE MANAGER, *wearing spectacles and assuming the role of Mr. Morgan, enters abruptly from the right and stands between the audience and the counter of his soda fountain.*

STAGE MANAGER.   Hello, George. Hello, Emily.—What'll you have?—Why, Emily Webb,—what you been crying about?

GEORGE.

He gropes for an explanation.

She . . . she just got an awful scare, Mr. Morgan. She almost got run over by that hardware-store wagon. Everybody says that Tom Huckins drives like a crazy man.

STAGE MANAGER.

Drawing a drink of water.

Well, now! You take a drink of water, Emily. You look all shook up. I tell you, you've got to look both ways before you cross Main Street these days. Gets worse every year.—What'll you have?

EMILY. I'll have a strawberry phosphate, thank you, Mr. Morgan.

GEORGE. No, no, Emily. Have an ice-cream soda with me. Two strawberry ice-cream sodas, Mr. Morgan.

STAGE MANAGER.

Working the faucets.

Two strawberry ice-cream sodas, yes sir. Yes, sir. There are a hundred and twenty-five horses in Grover's Corners this minute I'm talking to you. State Inspector was in here yesterday. And now they're bringing in these auto-mo-biles, the best thing to do is to just stay home. Why, I can remember when a dog could go to sleep all day in the middle of Main Street and nothing come along to disturb him.

He sets the imaginary glasses before them.

There they are. Enjoy 'em.

He sees a customer, right.

Yes, Mrs. Ellis. What can I do for you?

He goes out right.

EMILY. They're so expensive.

GEORGE. No, no,—don't you think of that. We're celebrating our election. And then do you know what else I'm celebrating?

EMILY. N-no.

GEORGE. I'm celebrating because I've got a friend who tells me all the things that ought to be told me.

EMILY. George, *please* don't think of that. I don't know why I said it. It's not true. You're—

GEORGE. No, Emily, you stick to it. I'm glad you spoke to me like you did. But you'll *see:* I'm going to change so quick—you bet I'm going to change. And, Emily, I want to ask you a favor.

EMILY. What?

GEORGE. Emily, if I go away to State Agriculture College next year, will you write me a letter once in a while?

EMILY. I certainly will. I certainly will, George . . .

Pause. They start sipping the sodas through the straws.

It certainly seems like being away three years you'd get out of touch with things. Maybe letters from Grover's Corners wouldn't be so interesting after a while. Grover's Corners isn't a very important place when you think of all—New Hampshire; but I think it's a very nice town.

GEORGE. The day wouldn't come when I wouldn't want to know everything that's happening here. I know *that's* true, Emily.

EMILY. Well, I'll try to make my letter interesting.

Pause.

GEORGE. Y'know. Emily, whenever I meet a farmer I ask him if he thinks it's important to go to Agriculture School to be a good farmer.

EMILY. Why, George—

GEORGE. Yeah, and some of them say that it's even a waste of time. You can get all those things, anyway, out of the pamphlets the government sends out. And Uncle Luke's getting old,—he's about ready for me to start in taking over this farm tomorrow, if I could.

EMILY. My!

GEORGE. And, like you say, being gone all that time . . . in other places and meeting other people . . . Gosh, if anything like that can happen I don't want to go away. I guess new people aren't any better than old ones. I'll bet they almost never are. Emily . . . I feel that you're as good a friend as I've got. I don't need to go to meet the people in other towns.

EMILY. But, George, maybe it's very important for you to go and learn all that about—cattle judging and soils and those things. . . . Of course, I don't know.

GEORGE.

After a pause, very seriously.

Emily, I'm going to make up my mind right now. I won't go. I'll tell Pa about it tonight.

EMILY.   Why, George, I don't see why you have to decide right now. It's a whole year away.

GEORGE.   Emily, I'm glad you spoke to me about that . . . that fault in my character. What you said was right; but there was *one* thing wrong in it, and that was when you said that for a year I wasn't noticing people, and . . . you, for instance. Why, you say you were watching me when I did everything . . . I was doing the same about you all the time. Why, sure,—I always thought about you as one of the chief people I thought about. I always made sure where you were sitting on the bleachers, and who you were with, and for three days now I've been trying to walk home with you; but something's always got in the way. Yesterday I was standing over against the wall waiting for you, and you walked home with *Miss Corcoran*.

EMILY.   George! . . . Life's awful funny! How could I have known that? Why, I thought—

GEORGE.   Listen, Emily, I'm going to tell you why I'm not going to Agriculture School. I think that once you've found a person that you're very fond of . . . I mean a person who's fond of you, too, and likes you enough to be interested in your character . . . Well, I think that's just as important as college is, and even more so. That's what I think.

EMILY.   I think it's awfully important, too.

GEORGE.   Emily.

EMILY.   Y-yes, George.

GEORGE.   Emily, if I *do* improve and make a big change . . . would you be . . . I mean: *could* you be . . .

EMILY.   I . . . I am now; I always have been.

GEORGE.

   Pause.

So I guess this is an important talk we've been having.

EMILY.   Yes . . . yes.

GEORGE.

   Takes a deep breath and straightens his back.

Wait just a minute and I'll walk you home.

With mounting alarm he digs into his pockets for the money.

The STAGE MANAGER *enters, right.*

GEORGE, *deeply embarrassed, but direct, says to him:*

Mr. Morgan, I'll have to go home and get the money to pay you for this. It'll only take me a minute.

STAGE MANAGER.

Pretending to be affronted.

What's that? George Gibbs, do you mean to tell me—!

GEORGE. Yes, but I had reasons, Mr. Morgan.—Look, here's my gold watch to keep until I come back with the money.

STAGE MANAGER. That's all right. Keep your watch. I'll trust you.

GEORGE. I'll be back in five minutes.

STAGE MANAGER. I'll trust you ten years, George,—not a day over.—Got all over your shock, Emily?

EMILY. Yes, thank you, Mr. Morgan. It was nothing.

GEORGE.

Taking up the books from the counter.

I'm ready.

They walk in grave silence across the stage and pass through the trellis at the Webbs' back door and disappear.

The STAGE MANAGER *watches them go out, then turns to the audience, removing his spectacles.*

STAGE MANAGER. Well,—

He claps his hands as a signal.

Now we're ready to get on with the wedding.

He stands waiting while the set is prepared for the next scene.

STAGEHANDS *remove the chairs, tables and trellises from the Gibbs and Webb houses.*

They arrange the pews for the church in the center of the stage. The congregation will sit facing the back wall. The aisle of the church starts at the center of the back wall and comes toward the audience.

A small platform is placed against the back wall on which the STAGE MANAGER *will stand later, playing the minister.*

The image of a stained-glass window is cast from a lantern slide upon the back wall.

When all is ready the STAGE MANAGER *strolls to the center of the stage, down front, and, musingly, addresses the audience.*

There are a lot of things to be said about a wedding; there are a lot of thoughts that go on during a wedding.

We can't get them all into one wedding, naturally, and especially not into a wedding at Grover's Corners, where they're awfully plain and short.

In this wedding I play the minister. That gives me the right to say a few more things about it.

For a while now, the play gets pretty serious.

Y'see, some churches say that marriage is a sacrament. I don't quite know what that means, but I can guess. Like Mrs. Gibbs said a few minutes ago: People were made to live two-by-two.

This is a good wedding, but people are so put together that even at a good wedding there's a lot of confusion way down deep in people's minds and we thought that that ought to be in our play, too.

The real hero of this scene isn't on the stage at all, and you know who that is. It's like what one of those European fellas said: every child born into the world is nature's attempt to make a perfect human being. Well, we've seen nature pushing and contriving for some time now. We all know that nature's interested in quantity; but I think she's interested in quality, too,—that's why I'm in the ministry.

And don't forget all the other witnesses at this wedding,—the ancestors. Millions of them. Most of them set out to live two-by-two, also. Millions of them.

Well, that's all my sermon. 'Twan't very long, anyway.

The organ starts playing Handel's "Largo."

The congregation streams into the church and sits in silence.

Church bells are heard.

MRS. GIBBS *sits in the front row, the first seat on the aisle, the right section; next to her are* REBECCA *and* DR. GIBBS.

Across the aisle MRS. WEBB, WALLY *and* MR. WEBB. *A small choir takes its place, facing the audience under the stained-glass window.*

MRS. WEBB, *on the way to her place, turns back and speaks to the audience.*

MRS. WEBB. I don't know why on earth I should be crying. I suppose there's nothing to cry about. It came over me at breakfast this morning; there was Emily eating her breakfast as she's done for seventeen years and now she's going off to eat in someone else's house. I suppose that's it.

And Emily! She suddenly said: I can't eat another mouthful, and she put her head down on the table and *she* cried.

She starts toward her seat in the church, but turns back and adds:

Oh, I've got to say it: you know, there's something downright cruel about sending our girls out into marriage this way.

I hope some of her girl friends have told her a thing or two. It's cruel, I know, but I couldn't bring myself to say anything. I went into it blind as a bat myself.

In half-amused exasperation.

The whole world's wrong, that's what's the matter.

There they come.

She hurries to her place in the pew.

GEORGE *starts to come down the right aisle of the theatre, through the audience.*

Suddenly THREE MEMBERS *of his baseball team appear by the right proscenium pillar and start whistling and catcalling to him. They are dressed for the ball field.*

THE BASEBALL PLAYERS. Eh, George, George! Hast—yaow! Look at him, fellas—he looks scared to death. Yaow! George, don't look so innocent, you old geezer. We know what you're thinking. Don't disgrace the team, big boy. Whoo-oo-oo.

STAGE MANAGER. All right! All right! That'll do. That's enough of that.

Smiling, he pushes them off the stage. They lean back to shout a few more catcalls.

There used to be an awful lot of that kind of thing at weddings in the old days,—Rome, and later. We're more civilized now,—so they say.

The choir starts singing "Love Divine, All Love Excelling—." GEORGE has reached the stage. He stares at the congregation a moment, then takes a few steps of withdrawal, toward the right proscenium pillar. His mother, from the front row, seems to have felt his confusion. She leaves her seat and comes down the aisle quickly to him.

MRS. GIBBS.   George! George! What's the matter?

GEORGE.   Ma, I don't want to grow old. Why's everybody pushing me so?

MRS. GIBBS.   Why, George . . . you wanted it.

GEORGE.   No, Ma, listen to me—

MRS. GIBBS.   No, no, George,—you're a man now.

GEORGE.   Listen, Ma,—for the last time I ask you . . . All I want to do is to be a fella—

MRS. GIBBS.   George! If anyone should hear you! Now stop. Why, I'm ashamed of you!

GEORGE.

He comes to himself and looks over the scene.

What? Where's Emily?

MRS. GIBBS.

Relieved.

George! You gave me such a turn.

GEORGE.   Cheer up, Ma. I'm getting married.

MRS. GIBBS.   Let me catch my breath a minute.

GEORGE.

Comforting her.

Now, Ma, you save Thursday nights. Emily and I are coming over to dinner every Thursday night . . . you'll see. Ma, what are you crying for? Come on; we've got to get ready for this.

MRS. GIBBS, mastering her emotion, fixes his tie and whispers to him.

In the meantime, EMILY, in white and wearing her wedding veil, has come through the audience and mounted onto the stage. She too draws back, frightened, when she sees the congregation in the church. The choir begins: "Blessed Be the Tie That Binds."

EMILY. I never felt so alone in my whole life. And George over there, looking so . . . ! I *hate* him. I wish I were dead. Papa! Papa!

MR. WEBB.

Leaves his seat in the pews and comes toward her anxiously.

Emily! Emily! Now don't get upset. . . .

EMILY. But, Papa,—I don't want to get married. . . .

MR. WEBB. Sh—sh—Emily. Everything's all right.

EMILY. Why can't I stay for a while just as I am? Let's go away,—

MR. WEBB. No, no, Emily. Now stop and think a minute.

EMILY. Don't you remember that you used to say,—all the time you used to say—all the time: that I was *your* girl! There must be lots of places we can go to. I'll work for you. I could keep house.

MR. WEBB. Sh . . . You mustn't think of such things. You're just nervous, Emily.

He turns and calls:

George! George! Will you come here a minute?

He leads her toward George.

Why you're marrying the best young fellow in the world. George is a fine fellow.

EMILY. But Papa,—

MRS. GIBBS *returns unobtrusively to her seat.*

MR. WEBB *has one arm around his daughter. He places his hand on* GEORGE'S *shoulder.*

MR. WEBB. I'm giving away my daughter, George. Do you think you can take care of her?

GEORGE. Mr. Webb, I want to . . . I want to try. Emily, I'm going to do my best. I love you, Emily. I need you.

EMILY. Well, if you love me, help me. All I want is someone to love me.

GEORGE. I will, Emily. Emily, I'll try.

EMILY. And I mean for *ever*. Do you hear? For ever and ever.

They fall into each other's arms.

The March from Lohengrin *is heard.*

The STAGE MANAGER, *as* CLERGYMAN, *stands on the box, up center.*

MR. WEBB.   Come, they're waiting for us. Now you know it'll be all right. Come, quick.

George slips away and takes his place beside the STAGE MANAGER-CLERGYMAN.

EMILY *proceeds up the aisle on her father's arm.*

STAGE MANAGER.   Do you, George, take this woman, Emily, to be your wedded wife, to have . . .

MRS. SOAMES *has been sitting in the last row of the congregation.*

She now turns to her neighbors and speaks in a shrill voice. Her chatter drowns out the rest of the clergyman's words.

MRS. SOAMES.   Perfectly lovely wedding! Loveliest wedding I ever saw. Oh, I do love a good wedding, don't you? Doesn't she make a lovely bride?

GEORGE.   I do.

STAGE MANAGER.   Do you, Emily, take this man, George, to be your wedded husband,—

Again his further words are covered by those of MRS. SOAMES.

MRS. SOAMES.   Don't know *when* I've seen such a lovely wedding. But I always cry. Don't know why it is, but I always cry. I just like to see young people happy, don't you? Oh, I think it's lovely.

The ring.

The kiss.

The stage is suddenly arrested into silent tableau.

The STAGE MANAGER, *his eyes on the distance, as though to himself:*

STAGE MANAGER.   I've married over two hundred couples in my day.

Do I believe in it?

I don't know.

M. . . . marries N. . . . millions of them.

The cottage, the go-cart, the Sunday-afternoon drives in the Ford, the first rheumatism, the grandchildren, the second rheumatism, the deathbed, the reading of the will,—

He now looks at the audience for the first time, with a warm smile that removes any sense of cynicism from the next line.

Once in a thousand times it's interesting.

—Well, let's have Mendelssohn's "Wedding March"!

The organ picks up the March.

The BRIDE *and* GROOM *come down the aisle, radiant, but trying to be very dignified.*

MRS. SOAMES. Aren't they a lovely couple? Oh, I've never been to such a nice wedding. I'm sure they'll be happy. I always say: *happiness*, that's the great thing! The important thing is to be happy.

The BRIDE *and* GROOM *reach the steps leading into the audience. A bright light is thrown upon them. They descend into the auditorium and run up the aisle joyously.*

STAGE MANAGER. That's all the Second Act, folks. Ten minutes' intermission.

CURTAIN

Act III

During the intermission the audience has seen the stagehands arranging the stage. On the right-hand side, a little right of the center, ten or twelve ordinary chairs have been placed in three openly spaced rows facing the audience.

These are graves in the cemetery.

Toward the end of the intermission the ACTORS *enter and take their places. The front row contains: toward the center of the stage, an empty chair; then* MRS. GIBBS; SIMON STIMSON.

The second row contains, among others, MRS. SOAMES.

The third row has WALLY WEBB.

The dead do not turn their heads or their eyes to right or left, but they sit in a quiet without stiffness. When they speak their tone is matter-of-fact, without sentimentality and, above all, without lugubriousness.

The STAGE MANAGER *takes his accustomed place and waits for the house lights to go down.*

STAGE MANAGER.   This time nine years have gone by, friends—summer, 1913.

Gradual changes in Grover's Corners. Horses are getting rarer.

Farmers coming into town in Fords.

Everybody locks their house doors now at night. Ain't been any burglars in town yet, but everybody's heard about 'em.

You'd be surprised, though—on the whole, things don't change much around here.

This is certainly an important part of Grover's Corners. It's on a hilltop—a windy hilltop—lots of sky, lots of clouds,—often lots of sun and moon and stars.

You come up here, on a fine afternoon and you can see range on range of hills—awful blue they are—up there by Lake Sunapee and Lake Winnipesaukee . . . and way up, if you've got a glass, you can see the White Mountains and Mt. Washington—where North Conway and Conway is. And, of course, our favorite mountain, Mt. Monadnock, 's right here—and all these towns that lie around it: Jaffrey, 'n East Jaffrey, 'n Peterborough, 'n Dublin; and

Then pointing down in the audience.

there, quite a ways down, is Grover's Corners.

Yes, beautiful spot up here. Mountain laurel and li-lacks. I often wonder why people like to be buried in Woodlawn and Brooklyn when they might pass the same time up here in New Hampshire.

Over there—

Pointing to stage left.

are the old stones,—1670, 1680. Strong-minded people that come a long way to be independent. Summer people walk around there laughing at the funny words on the tombstones . . . it don't do any harm. And genealogists come up from Boston—get paid by city people for looking up their ancestors. They want to make sure they're Daughters of the American Revolution and of the *Mayflower.* . . . Well, I guess that don't do any harm, either. Wherever you come near the human race, there's layers and layers of nonsense. . . .

Over there are some Civil War veterans. Iron flags on their graves . . . New Hampshire boys . . . had a notion that the Union ought to be kept together, though they'd never seen more than fifty miles of it themselves. All they knew was the name, friends—the United States of America. The United States of America. And they went and died about it.

This here is the new part of the cemetery. Here's your friend Mrs. Gibbs. 'N let me see—Here's Mr. Stimson, organist at the Congregational Church. And Mrs. Soames who enjoyed the wedding so—you remember? Oh, and a lot of others. And Editor Webb's boy, Wallace, whose appendix burst while he was on a Boy Scout trip to Crawford Notch.

Yes, an awful lot of sorrow has sort of quieted down up here.

People just wild with grief have brought their relatives up to this hill. We all know how it is . . . and then time . . . and sunny days . . . and rainy days . . . 'n snow . . . We're all glad they're in a beautiful place and we're coming up here ourselves when our fit's over.

Now there are some things we all know, but we don't take'm out and look at'm very often. We all know that *something* is eternal. And it ain't houses and it ain't names, and it ain't earth, and it ain't even the stars . . . everybody knows in their bones that *something* is eternal, and that something has to do with human beings. All the greatest people ever lived have been telling us that for five thousand years and yet you'd be surprised how people are always losing hold of it. There's something way down deep that's eternal about every human being.

Pause.

You know as well as I do that the dead don't stay interested in us living people for very long. Gradually, gradually, they lose hold of the earth . . . and the ambitions they had . . . and the pleasures they had . . . and the things they suffered . . . and the people they loved.

They get weaned away from earth—that's the way I put it,—weaned away.

And they stay here while the earth part of 'em burns away, burns out; and all that time they slowly get indifferent to what's goin' on in Grover's Corners.

They're waitin'. They're waitin' for something that they feel is comin'. Something important, and great. Aren't they waitin' for the eternal part in them to come out clear?

Some of the things they're going to say maybe'll hurt your feelings—but that's the way it is: mother'n daughter . . . husband 'n wife . . . enemy 'n enemy . . . money 'n miser . . . all those terribly important things kind of grow pale around here. And what's left when memory's gone, and your identity, Mrs. Smith?

He looks at the audience a minute, then turns to the stage.

Well! There are some *living* people. There's Joe Stoddard, our undertaker, supervising a new-made grave. And here comes a Grover's Corners boy, that left town to go out West.

JOE STODDARD *has hovered about in the background.* SAM CRAIG *enters left, wiping his forehead from the exertion. He carries an umbrella and strolls front.*

SAM CRAIG.   Good afternoon, Joe Stoddard.

JOE STODDARD.   Good afternoon, good afternoon. Let me see now: do I know you?

SAM CRAIG.   I'm Sam Craig.

JOE STODDARD.   Gracious sakes' alive! Of all people! I should'a knowed you'd be back for the funeral. You've been away a long time, Sam.

SAM CRAIG.   Yes, I've been away over twelve years. I'm in business out in Buffalo now, Joe. But I was in the East when I got news of my cousin's death, so I thought I'd combine things a little and come and see the old home. You look well.

JOE STODDARD. Yes, yes, can't complain. Very sad, our journey today, Samuel.

SAM CRAIG. Yes.

JOE STODDARD. Yes, yes. I always say I hate to supervise when a young person is taken. They'll be here in a few minutes now. I had to come here early today—my son's supervisin' at the home.

SAM CRAIG.

Reading stones.

Old Farmer McCarty, I used to do chores for him—after school. He had the lumbago.

JOE STODDARD. Yes, we brought Farmer McCarty here a number of years ago now.

SAM CRAIG.

Staring at Mrs. Gibbs' knees.

Why, this is my Aunt Julia . . . I'd forgotten that she'd . . . of course, of course.

JOE STODDARD. Yes, Doc Gibbs lost his wife two-three years ago . . . about this time. And today's another pretty bad blow for him, too.

MRS. GIBBS.

To Simon Stimson: in an even voice.

That's my sister Carey's boy, Sam . . . Sam Craig.

SIMON STIMSON. I'm always uncomfortable when *they're* around.

MRS. GIBBS. Simon.

SAM CRAIG. Do they choose their own verses much, Joe?

JOE STODDARD. No . . . not usual. Mostly the bereaved pick a verse.

SAM CRAIG. Doesn't sound like Aunt Julia. There aren't many of those Hersey sisters left now. Let me see: where are . . . I wanted to look at my father's and mother's . . .

JOE STODDARD. Over there with the Craigs . . . Avenue F.

SAM CRAIG.

Reading Simon Stimson's epitaph.

He was organist at church, wasn't he?—Hm, drank a lot, we used to say.

JOE STODDARD. Nobody was supposed to know about it. He'd seen a peck of trouble.

Behind his hand.

Took his own life, y' know?

SAM CRAIG. Oh, did he?

JOE STODDARD. Hung himself in the attic. They tried to hush it up, but of course it got around. He chose his own epy-taph. You can see it there. It ain't a verse exactly.

SAM CRAIG. Why, it's just some notes of music—what is it?

JOE STODDARD. Oh, I wouldn't know. It was wrote up in the Boston papers at the time.

SAM CRAIG. Joe, what did she die of?

JOE STODDARD. Who?

SAM CRAIG. My cousin.

JOE STODDARD. Oh, didn't you know? Had some trouble bringing a baby into the world. 'Twas her second, though. There's a little boy 'bout four years old.

SAM CRAIG.

Opening his umbrella.

The grave's going to be over there?

JOE STODDARD. Yes, there ain't much more room over here among the Gibbses, so they're opening up a whole new Gibbs section over by Avenue B. You'll excuse me now. I see they're comin'.

From left to center, at the back of the stage, comes a procession. FOUR MEN *carry a casket, invisible to us. All the rest are under umbrellas. One can vaguely see:* DR. GIBBS, GEORGE, *the* WEBBS, *etc. They gather about a grave in the back center of the stage, a little to the left of center.*

MRS. SOAMES. Who is it, Julia?

MRS. GIBBS.

Without raising her eyes.

My daughter-in-law, Emily Webb.

MRS. SOAMES.

A little surprised, but no emotion.

Well, I declare! The road up here must have been awfully muddy. What did she die of, Julia?

MRS. GIBBS. In childbirth.

MRS. SOAMES. Childbirth.

Almost with a laugh.

I'd forgotten all about that. My, wasn't life awful—

With a sigh.

and wonderful.

SIMON STIMSON.

With a sideways glance.

Wonderful, was it?

MRS. GIBBS. Simon! Now, remember!

MRS. SOAMES. I remember Emily's wedding. Wasn't it a lovely wedding! And I remember her reading the class poem at Graduation Exercises. Emily was one of the brightest girls ever graduated from High School. I've heard Principal Wilkins say so time after time. I called on them at their new farm, just before I died. Perfectly beautiful farm.

A WOMAN FROM AMONG THE DEAD. It's on the same road we lived on.

A MAN AMONG THE DEAD. Yepp, right smart farm.

They subside. The group by the grave starts singing "Blessed Be the Tie That Binds."

A WOMAN AMONG THE DEAD. I always liked that hymn. I was hopin' they'd sing a hymn.

Pause. Suddenly EMILY *appears from among the umbrellas. She is wearing a white dress. Her hair is down her back and tied by a white ribbon like a little girl. She comes slowly, gazing wonderingly at the dead, a little dazed.*

She stops halfway and smiles faintly. After looking at the mourners for a moment, she walks slowly to the vacant chair beside Mrs. Gibbs and sits down.

EMILY.

To them all, quietly, smiling.

Hello.

MRS. SOAMES. Hello, Emily.

A MAN AMONG THE DEAD Hello, M's Gibbs.

EMILY.

Warmly.

Hello, Mother Gibbs.

MRS. GIBBS. Emily.

EMILY. Hello.

With surprise.

It's raining.

Her eyes drift back to the funeral company.

MRS. GIBBS. Yes . . . They'll be gone soon, dear. Just rest yourself.

EMILY. It seems thousands and thousands of years since I . . . Papa remembered that that was my favorite hymn.

Oh, I wish I'd been here a long time. I don't like being new here.—How do you do, Mr. Stimson?

SIMON STIMSON. How do you do, Emily.

EMILY continues to look about her with a wondering smile; as though to shut out from her mind the thought of the funeral company she starts speaking to Mrs. Gibbs with a touch of nervousness.

EMILY. Mother Gibbs, George and I have made that farm into just the best place you ever saw. We thought of you all the time. We wanted to show you the new barn and a great long ce-ment drinking fountain for the stock. We bought that out of the money you left us.

MRS. GIBBS. I did?

EMILY. Don't you remember, Mother Gibbs—the legacy you left us? Why, it was over three hundred and fifty dollars.

MRS. GIBBS. Yes, yes, Emily.

EMILY. Well, there's a patent device on the drinking fountain so that it never overflows, Mother Gibbs, and it never sinks below a certain mark they have there. It's fine.

Her voice trails off and her eyes return to the funeral group.

It won't be the same to George without me, but it's a lovely farm.

Suddenly she looks directly at Mrs. Gibbs.

Live people don't understand, do they?

MRS. GIBBS. No, dear—not very much.

EMILY. They're sort of shut up in little boxes, aren't they? I feel as though I knew them last a thousand years ago . . . My boy is spending the day at Mrs. Carter's.

She sees MR. CARTER *among the dead.*

Oh, Mr. Carter, my little boy is spending the day at your house.

MR. CARTER. Is he?

EMILY. Yes, he loves it there.—Mother Gibbs, we have a Ford, too. Never gives us any trouble. I don't drive, though. Mother Gibbs, when does this feeling go away?—Of being . . . one of *them*? How long does it . . . ?

MRS. GIBBS. Sh! dear. Just wait and be patient.

EMILY.

With a sigh.

I know.—Look, they're finished. They're going.

MRS. GIBBS. Sh—.

The umbrellas leave the stage. DR. GIBBS *has come over to his wife's grave and stands before it a moment.* EMILY *looks up at his face.* MRS. GIBBS *does not raise her eyes.*

EMILY. Look! Father Gibbs is bringing some of my flowers to you. He looks just like George, doesn't he? Oh, Mother Gibbs, I never realized before how troubled and how . . . how in the dark live persons are. Look at him. I loved him so. From morning till night, that's all they are—troubled.

DR. GIBBS *goes off.*

THE DEAD. Little cooler than it was.—Yes, that rain's cooled it off a little. Those northeast winds always do the same thing, don't they? If it isn't rain, it's a three-day blow.—

A patient calm falls on the stage. The STAGE MANAGER *appears at his proscenium pillar, smoking.* EMILY *sits up abruptly with an idea.*

EMILY. But, Mother Gibbs, one can go back; one can go back there again . . . into living. I feel it. I know it. Why just then for a moment I was thinking about . . . about the farm . . . and for a minute I *was* there, and my baby was on my lap as plain as day.

MRS. GIBBS. Yes, of course you can.

EMILY. I can go back there and live all those days over again . . . why not?

MRS. GIBBS. All I can say is, Emily, don't.

EMILY.

She appeals urgently to the stage manager.

But it's true, isn't it? I can go and live . . . back there . . . again.

STAGE MANAGER. Yes, some have tried—but they soon come back here.

MRS. GIBBS. Don't do it, Emily.

MRS. SOAMES. Emily, don't. It's not what you think it'd be.

EMILY. But I won't live over a sad day. I'll choose a happy one—I'll choose the day I first knew that I loved George. Why should that be painful?

THEY *are silent. Her question turns to the stage manager.*

STAGE MANAGER. You not only live it; but you watch yourself living it.

EMILY. Yes?

STAGE MANAGER. And as you watch it, you see the thing that they—down there—never know. You see the future. You know what's going to happen afterwards.

EMILY. But is that—painful? Why?

MRS. GIBBS. That's not the only reason why you shouldn't do it, Emily. When you've been here longer you'll see that our life here is to forget all that, and think only of what's ahead, and be ready for what's ahead. When you've been here longer you'll understand.

EMILY.

Softly.

But, Mother Gibbs, how can I *ever* forget that life? It's all I know. It's all I had.

MRS. SOAMES.   Oh, Emily. It isn't wise. Really, it isn't.

EMILY.   But it's a thing I must know for myself. I'll choose a happy day, anyway.

MRS. GIBBS.   *No!*—At least, choose an unimportant day. Choose the least important day in your life. It will be important enough.

EMILY.

To herself.

Then it can't be since I was married; or since the baby was born.

To the stage manager, eagerly.

I can choose a birthday at least, can't I?—I choose my twelfth birthday.

STAGE MANAGER.   All right. February 11th, 1899. A Tuesday.—Do you want any special time of day?

EMILY.   Oh, I want the whole day.

STAGE MANAGER.   We'll begin at dawn. You remember it had been snowing for several days; but it had stopped the night before, and they had begun clearing the roads. The sun's coming up.

EMILY.

With a cry; rising.

There's Main Street . . . why, that's Mr. Morgan's drugstore before he changed it! . . . And there's the livery stable.

The stage at no time in this act has been very dark; but now the left half of the stage gradually becomes very bright—the brightness of a crisp winter morning. EMILY *walks toward Main Street.*

STAGE MANAGER.   Yes, it's 1899. This is fourteen years ago.

EMILY.   Oh, that's the town I knew as a little girl. And, *look*, there's the old white fence that used to be around our house. Oh, I'd forgotten that! Oh, I love it so! Are they inside?

STAGE MANAGER. Yes, your mother'll be coming downstairs in a minute to make breakfast.

EMILY.

Softly.

Will she?

STAGE MANAGER. And you remember: your father had been away for several days; he came back on the early-morning train.

EMILY. No . . . ?

STAGE MANAGER. He'd been back to his college to make a speech—in western New York, at Clinton.

EMILY. Look! There's Howie Newsome. There's our policeman. But he's *dead; he died.*

The voices of HOWIE NEWSOME, CONSTABLE WARREN *and* JOE CROWELL, JR., *are heard at the left of the stage.* EMILY *listens in delight.*

HOWIE NEWSOME. Whoa, Bessie!—Bessie! 'Morning, Bill.

CONSTABLE WARREN. Morning, Howie.

HOWIE NEWSOME. You're up early.

CONSTABLE WARREN. Been rescuin' a party; darn near froze to death, down by Polish Town thar. Got drunk and lay out in the snowdrifts. Thought he was in bed when I shook'm.

EMILY. Why, there's Joe Crowell . . .

JOE CROWELL. Good morning, Mr. Warren. 'Morning, Howie.

MRS. WEBB *has appeared in her kitchen, but* EMILY *does not see her until she calls.*

MRS. WEBB. Chil-*dren!* Wally! Emily! . . . Time to get up.

EMILY. Mama, I'm here! Oh! how young Mama looks! I didn't know Mama was ever that young.

MRS. WEBB. You can come and dress by the kitchen fire, if you like; but hurry.

HOWIE NEWSOME *has entered along Main Street and brings the milk to Mrs. Webb's door.*

Good morning, Mr. Newsome. Whhhh—it's cold.

HOWIE NEWSOME. Ten below by my barn, Mrs. Webb.

MRS. WEBB. Think of it! Keep yourself wrapped up.

She takes her bottles in, shuddering.

EMILY.

With an effort.

Mama, I can't find my blue hair ribbon anywhere.

MRS. WEBB. Just open your eyes, dear, that's all. I laid it out for you special—on the dresser, there. If it were a snake it would bite you.

EMILY. Yes, yes . . .

She puts her hand on her heart. MR. WEBB *comes along Main Street, where he meets* CONSTABLE WARREN. *Their movements and voices are increasingly lively in the sharp air.*

MR. WEBB. Good morning, Bill.

CONSTABLE WARREN. Good morning, Mr. Webb. You're up early.

MR. WEBB. Yes, just been back to my old college in New York State. Been any trouble here?

CONSTABLE WARREN. Well, I was called up this mornin' to rescue a Polish fella—darn near froze to death he was.

MR. WEBB. We must get it in the paper.

CONSTABLE WARREN. 'Twan't much.

EMILY.

Whispers.

Papa.

MR. WEBB *shakes the snow off his feet and enters his house.* CONSTABLE WARREN *goes off, right.*

MR. WEBB. Good morning, Mother.

MRS. WEBB. How did it go, Charles?

MR. WEBB. Oh, fine, I guess. I told'm a few things.—Everything all right here?

MRS. WEBB. Yes—can't think of anything that's happened, special. Been right cold. Howie Newsome says it's ten below over to his barn.

MR. WEBB. Yes, well, it's colder than that at Hamilton College. Students' ears are falling off. It ain't Christian.—Paper have any mistakes in it?

MRS. WEBB. None that I noticed. Coffee's ready when you want it.

He starts upstairs.

Charles! Don't forget, it's Emily's birthday. Did you remember to get her something?

MR. WEBB.

Patting his pocket.

Yes, I've got something here.

Calling up the stairs.

Where's my girl? Where's my birthday girl?

He goes off left.

MRS. WEBB. Don't interrupt her now, Charles. You can see her at breakfast. She's slow enough as it is. Hurry up, children! It's seven o'clock. Now, I don't want to call you again.

EMILY.

Softly, more in wonder than in grief.

I can't bear it. They're so young and beautiful. Why did they ever have to get old? Mama, I'm here. I'm grown up. I love you all, everything.—I can't look at everything hard enough.

She looks questioningly at the STAGE MANAGER, *saying or suggesting: "Can I go in?" He nods briefly. She crosses to the inner door to the kitchen, left of her mother, and as though entering the room, says, suggesting the voice of a girl of twelve.*

Good morning, Mama.

MRS. WEBB.

Crossing to embrace and kiss her; in her characteristic matter-of-fact manner.

Well, now, dear, a very happy birthday to my girl and many happy returns. There are some surprises waiting for you on the kitchen table.

EMILY. Oh, Mama, you *shouldn't* have.

She throws an anguished glance at the stage manager.

I can't—I can't.

MRS. WEBB.

Facing the audience, over her stove.

But birthday or no birthday, I want you to eat your breakfast good and slow. I want you to grow up and be a good strong girl.

That in the blue paper is from your Aunt Carrie; and I reckon you can guess who brought the post-card album. I found it on the doorstep when I brought in the milk—George Gibbs . . . must have come over in the cold pretty early . . . right nice of him.

EMILY.

To herself.

Oh, George! I'd forgotten that. . . .

MRS. WEBB.   Chew that bacon good and slow. It'll help keep you warm on a cold day.

EMILY.

With mounting urgency.

Oh, Mama, just look at me one minute as though you really saw me. Mama, fourteen years have gone by. I'm dead. You're a grandmother, Mama. I married George Gibbs, Mama. Wally's dead, too. Mama, his appendix burst on a camping trip to North Conway. We felt just terrible about it—don't you remember? But, just for a moment now we're all together. Mama, just for a moment we're happy. *Let's look at one another.*

MRS. WEBB.   That in the yellow paper is something I found in the attic among your grandmother's things. You're old enough to wear it now, and I thought you'd like it.

EMILY.   And this is from you. Why, Mama, it's just lovely and it's just what I wanted. It's beautiful!

She flings her arms around her mother's neck. Her MOTHER *goes on with her cooking, but is pleased.*

MRS. WEBB.   Well, I hoped you'd like it. Hunted all over. Your Aunt Norah couldn't find one in Concord, so I had to send all the way to Boston.

Laughing.

Wally has something for you, too. He made it at manual-training class and he's very proud of it. Be sure you make a big fuss about it.—Your father has a surprise for you, too; don't know what it is myself. Sh—here he comes.

MR. WEBB.

Off stage.

Where's my girl? Where's my birthday girl?

EMILY.

In a loud voice to the stage manager.

I can't. I can't go on. It goes so fast. We don't have time to look at one another.

She breaks down sobbing.

The lights dim on the left half of the stage. MRS. WEBB *disappears.*

I didn't realize. So all that was going on and we never noticed. Take me back—up the hill—to my grave. But first: Wait! One more look.

Good-by, Good-by, world. Good-by, Grover's Corners . . . Mama and Papa. Good-by to clocks ticking . . . and Mama's sunflowers. And food and coffee. And new-ironed dresses and hot baths . . . and sleeping and waking up. Oh, earth, you're too wonderful for anybody to realize you.

She looks toward the stage manager and asks abruptly, through her tears:

Do any human beings ever realize life while they live it?—every, every minute?

STAGE MANAGER. No.

Pause.

The saints and poets, maybe—they do some.

EMILY. I'm ready to go back.

She returns to her chair beside Mrs. Gibbs.

Pause.

MRS. GIBBS. Were you happy?

EMILY. No . . . I should have listened to you. That's all human beings are! Just blind people.

MRS. GIBBS. Look, it's clearing up. The stars are coming out.

EMILY. Oh, Mr. Stimson, I should have listened to them.

SIMON STIMSON.

With mounting violence; bitingly.

Yes, now you know. Now you know! That's what it was to be alive. To move about in a cloud of ignorance; to go up and down trampling on the feelings of those . . . of those about you. To spend and waste time as though you had a million years. To be always at the mercy of one self-centered passion, or another. Now you know—that's the happy existence you wanted to go back to. Ignorance and blindness.

MRS. GIBBS.

Spiritedly.

Simon Stimson, that ain't the whole truth and you know it. Emily, look at that star. I forget its name.

A MAN AMONG THE DEAD. My boy Joel was a sailor,—knew 'em all. He'd set on the porch evenings and tell 'em all by name. Yes, sir, wonderful!

ANOTHER MAN AMONG THE DEAD. A star's mighty good company.

A WOMAN AMONG THE DEAD. Yes, yes, 'tis.

SIMON STIMSON. Here's one of *them* coming.

THE DEAD. That's funny. 'Tain't no time for one of them to be here.— Goodness sakes.

EMILY. Mother Gibbs, it's George.

MRS. GIBBS. Sh, dear. Just rest yourself.

EMILY. It's George.

GEORGE *enters from the left, and slowly comes toward them.*

A MAN FROM AMONG THE DEAD. And my boy, Joel, who knew the stars—he used to say it took millions of years for that speck o' light to git to the earth. Don't seem like a body could believe it, but that's what he used to say— millions of years.

GEORGE *sinks to his knees then falls full length at Emily's feet.*

A WOMAN AMONG THE DEAD. Goodness! That ain't no way to behave!

MRS. SOAMES. He ought to be home.

EMILY. Mother Gibbs?

MRS. GIBBS. Yes, Emily?

EMILY. They don't understand, do they?

MRS. GIBBS. No, dear. They don't understand.

The STAGE MANAGER *appears at the right, one hand on a dark curtain which he slowly draws across the scene.*

In the distance a clock is heard striking the hour very faintly.

STAGE MANAGER. Most everybody's asleep in Grover's Corners. There are a few lights on: Shorty Hawkins, down at the depot, has just watched the Albany train go by. And at the livery stable somebody's setting up late and talking.—Yes, it's clearing up. There are the stars—doing their old, old crisscross journeys in the sky. Scholars haven't settled the matter yet, but they seem to think there are no living beings up there. Just chalk . . . or fire. Only this one is straining away, straining away all the time to make something of itself. The strain's so bad that every sixteen hours everybody lies down and gets a rest.

He winds his watch.

Hm. . . . Eleven o'clock in Grover's Corners.—You get a good rest, too. Good night.

THE END

Related Readings

Carolyn Meyer

from
White Lilacs

*Carolyn Meyer's novel is told from the point of view of
a teenage girl who lives in Freedomtown, the African-
American section of a Texas town, in 1921.*

GRANDFATHER AND I walked home together. I wasn't too old yet to
hold onto his hand. We followed the old trolley tracks east on Oak Street,
past the fine houses that were Mr. and Mrs. Bell's neighbors', past the courthouse with the clock that chimed the hour loud enough for us all to hear,
and north across Brown Street to Freedomtown.

You knew soon as you crossed Brown Street that you were in a different
place. Hickory Creek was still swollen from spring rains. The three streets
that ran north and south and the three streets that cut east and west across
them were not paved (they were muddy now from where the two branches
of Hickory Creek crossed over, but later, as the summer wore on, my bare
feet would be buried in warm dust). Most all the houses were small and
plain, without a lick of paint, and set close together. Some might say they
looked poor, but each and every one had some little bit of something color-
ful growing in the front yard. Nothing like Grandfather Jim's, but then that
was a special case. You could have only one Garden of Eden.

Hand in hand we walked up Logan Street, our main street with Booker
T. Washington Colored School at one end by Brown Street and Forgiveness
Baptist Church where my whole family belonged clear up at the other end
by Academy Street. . . .

I was born in Freedomtown. So was my mother, but all the old people
had a story to tell about how they came to be there. Grandmother Lila was a
young girl when her family, the Huckabys, moved with a group of other families from near Dallas and helped to establish the little settlement in Dillon
during Reconstruction, which followed the War Between the States.

Grandfather Jim had a different story: his poppa was a white man who
brought his momma who was once a slave woman all the way out here from
Virginia. He bought her a piece of land right next to his own farm up near
Blue Springs. That white man acknowledged Grandfather as his son all
along and gave Grandfather's momma money for him and her other children

by him, but then he died young and Grandfather had to move to town to get work to support his mother and sisters.

When Grandfather and Grandmother married, they settled in Freedom, and most of their family still lived there: Aunt Tillie was the oldest, and then Uncle Theo, who was married to Aunt Flora, and then Momma. Uncle Walter, the youngest, was married to Aunt Vinnie.

My grandfather on Poppa's side was part Seminole, but I never knew him. Poppa came from East Texas when he was a boy with his father and an uncle and one of Poppa's brothers, looking for land to farm. Only Poppa ended up staying in Freedom, and the others went on west. His momma stayed back in East Texas and got a new husband. We used to hear now and then from Poppa's youngest sister, who went to college and was a school-teacher in St. Louis. This Aunt Susannah came to visit us once when I was barely three years old, but I didn't remember her.

"We got all kinds in my family," Poppa used to say, and I knew that idea tickled him.

"Sure do," Momma would reply in a way that made me know she didn't entirely approve of families splitting up, some going, some staying.

My father owned a barbershop, and my mother took in washing for Mrs. Bell and some other white ladies. Momma wanted me to help out with her laundry business, but I disliked that, preferring to do my helping out in Mrs. Bell's garden. She didn't pay me for my work, but Grandfather gave me a little something out of his pocket for the time I spent there. Whenever I was not in school, I could be found at Mrs. Bell's with Grandfather.

Some of the people of Freedomtown worked at the flour mill or the brickyard. Some, like Poppa and a dozen others, had their own businesses. Others worked at the Dillon Academy for Young Ladies, a finishing school for white girls, with fine brick buildings and green lawns just north of Freedomtown. When the wind was right, we could hear their voices in their playing field on the other side of Academy Street, within sight of Forgiveness Baptist Church.

Most of the rest of our people were employed in the homes of rich folks like Mr. and Mrs. Bell on the west side of Dillon, where the houses were very grand and help was needed to clean and cook and serve and take care of the gardens and mind the children. In fact, the rich folks of Dillon could be counted on to give work to most anybody who wanted it. A few, like my brother Henry, refused to work for them, no matter what the job. . . .

It was suppertime as Grandfather Jim and I walked up Logan Street, and I could smell the cooking. Most of the children had been called inside. Otherwise it would have been noisy and hectic with dozens of little kids, in-cluding my two young sisters, Lora Lee and Nancy Lee, running around, laughing and playing with the others. I knew them all. Grandmother Lila was a midwife who had delivered most of the babies in Freedomtown, sometimes taking care of them when their mommas went back to work. I remembered when I used to be like that, young and carefree, having only to mind my momma and not worry about a thing except when I was going to have a chance to play with my friends. But today I felt about a hundred years old, ever since I heard some ladies talking at the Garden Club luncheon about how they were going to make us move away from Freedomtown.

If Grandfather's Garden of Eden was my favorite place in Freedom, my next favorite was Grandmother's parlor, where she sat in her big old rocking chair and did her fancywork after whatever baby she was minding had gone to sleep. A second rocking chair was always ready and waiting for a visitor, and I went there whenever I could. That evening when we entered the house she was sitting in her chair with a neighbor's colicky baby who she was caring for. It screeched so loud in spite of the rocking I couldn't hear myself think. I decided to go on up Logan Street to my own house. Grandmother called, "Come back tomorrow, Rose Lee." Grandfather said he'd walk along with me. I wasn't surprised.

Our home was stark by comparison. My parents didn't have time or interest in growing anything we couldn't eat, and the yard behind our plain wooden house was strung with clotheslines like the warp of a loom with only a small garden patch in the corner opposite the privy for a few melons and some okra. Even so, wild hollyhocks stood tall along the veranda, and Grandfather had brought over some petunias to plant by the steps. He couldn't stand to see a yard that wasn't blooming somehow.

My father was busy in his barbershop in the front room of our house. He stayed open most evenings right through the supper hour, when his customers had time after their work was done to sit down for a visit as well as a shave and a haircut. When it was warm, as it was that night, the men waited their turn out on the veranda, tipping straight wooden chairs back against the house wall or lounging on the wide steps, carrying on their talk through the open window with whoever was inside.

I liked to stay around my father's barbershop, listening to the men talk. I overheard lots of interesting stories there, although my mother did not approve. Not the proper place for a young lady, who might hear bad language and other things that weren't intended for her ears, she claimed.

The evening after the Garden Club lunch I stopped in the barbershop before I went on through to tell Momma I was home. A customer was seated in the barber chair, draped with a clean white towel, and another half dozen men waited their turns.

I recognized all of Poppa's customers: Mr. Morgan, the undertaker, said to be the wealthiest man in Freedom. ("Why not?" my grandmother said. "Everybody needs him sooner or later.") Mr. Lipscomb, who owned a boardinghouse. Pastor Mobley, preacher at Forgiveness Baptist Church. Mr. Ross, head janitor at the Academy. Mr. Webster, proprietor of the Sun-Up Café where the men also gathered to sit and talk, cups of coffee in their hands, while the big slow fan turned noisily overhead. Most of the important men of Freedom were waiting while my father snipped away at the undertaker's bowed head.

Grandfather greeted those on the veranda and followed me inside. "Tell them what you heard, Rose Lee," he said.

My mouth went dry, with all of them looking at me. My father's scissors hovered in mid-air. "They want to move us," I said. "The ladies of the Dillon Garden Club were saying at Mrs. Bell's that they want to make us all move away somewhere so they can turn Freedom into a park."

Mr. Webster swore, the kind of language my mother didn't approve of and was afraid I'd hear at the barbershop, and then he apologized to me and to the preacher. "What have I been telling you?" Mr. Webster went on, looking from one to the next. "Isn't this exactly the rumor we been hearing and pretending not to hear? And is it not time to believe it, now that this child has brought us the word, and to figure out what it is we're going to do?"

The men muttered. I saw heads nodding.

"What all did you hear them say, Rose Lee?" Poppa interrupted in his soft, growly voice. "Try to remember everything."

Those who were outside crowded into the little shop to listen better. I repeated every detail that came to mind, mentioning this time the lady from up North who spoke in a different way. "She was the only one who thought we might not like to be moved," I told them.

After they had all asked questions and made me repeat everything I already told them, they began to discuss it among themselves, seeming to forget I was there. That was all right—I preferred to listen anyhow.

Poppa whisked Mr. Morgan's face and neck with a soft-bristled brush and shook the hairs off the white towel, and Mr. Morgan stepped down out of the barber chair and Pastor Mobley took his place. But the undertaker didn't leave; he settled into the chair the preacher had been waiting in.

When a new customer arrived, the men made room for him. More came, but nobody left. When there was no more room inside, they clustered outside the open window. They all wanted to discuss the news I had brought concerning the Garden Club and its plans to beautify Dillon by getting rid of us.

"What are we going to do?" asked one of the men.

"We'll make our voices heard," said Poppa in his growly voice. "We'll tell them it's our property, legally bought and paid for, papers to prove it." He pulled himself up straight and proud, and he gripped his scissors like a sword.

"We'll tell them we're not leaving. What can they do about it?"

One of the men, Mr. Ross I think it was, chuckled softly. "Do whatever they've a mind to, Charlie. You know that."

My brother Henry had come through the heavy green curtain that separated the barbershop from the rest of our house and stood with his arms folded across his chest. He was tall and handsome with Indian features like Poppa's.

"We'll fight it, that's what we're going to do," Henry said in a deep voice like Poppa's, but younger sounding. "We'll do whatever we have to. They have no right."

"Won't do any good to fight it," Mr. Webster said. "You can say all you like, but if they decide to knock down our homes to make their park, then you can bet there will be a park right where we're standing."

The men stayed late, way past the time Poppa generally locked the front door and passed to the other side of the green curtain for the supper Momma had been keeping warm for him. Some agreed with my father— they would fight to save Freedomtown. Others felt it was useless and were mainly concerned about where they would go when they had to leave.

Then my momma came to get me, annoyed that I wasn't helping back in the kitchen, starting off with her usual. "Rose Lee, how many times do I have to tell you—"

"Listen, Momma," I said, made bold by the attention paid me by my father's customers, "this is what I heard." And I repeated the story one more time. I felt proud to be carrying such important news, proud that Poppa was going to make our voices heard and Henry was going to fight, and if I knew Grandfather Jim, he wouldn't be sitting quietly while they chased him out of his own Garden of Eden.

But Momma didn't look as though she was ready for any fight. My mother burst into tears and cried in front of all those men. That was not the only time she cried in the months that followed.

* * *

One by one our houses were hauled away to The Flats. It was a sight nearly everybody turned out to watch. Most of the able-bodied men of Freedom gathered to help. This took place at night when the roads around Dillon were empty of traffic, and those who weren't taking their spell of helping held torches to light the way for those who were.

First they jacked up the house and set wooden runners under it. Then they shoved logs under the runners and hitched the runners to a team of mules, hired from a farmer out near Grover Point and paid for by the city, like they promised. The mule driver clucked his tongue and the mules leaned against the weight of their burden until slowly the house began to roll on the logs. Quickly the men rushed around to the back, grabbed the last log as the runners passed over it, and scrambled to lay that log in front. They did this over and over again as the house inched slowly toward its new site.

The night it was time for our house to go, Momma sent my little sisters and me to stay with Grandmother Lila. Nancy Lee and Lora Lee fell asleep right away in Grandmother's big bed, but I knew there would be no sleep for me that night.

I tried to sketch the scene as our house crept slowly down Logan Street past Grandmother's parlor window, but my figures of men and mules held little resemblance to the real thing. I was about to give up trying when Grandmother Lila laid aside the album quilt she was piecing for Dr. Ragsdale's family, a Bible verse stitched on each square by one of his patients. She peered through her glasses at my drawing of the scene.

"Oh, don't look," I begged. "I can't do people or animals."

"You do them good enough to help us remember," she said, so I kept on with it until I got too tired.

That was the last drawing I would do of Freedom.

The next day I stayed home from school to help Momma unpack, trying to put everything back exactly the way it was. That night I climbed into bed next to my sisters and fell asleep, all worn out. I hung Miss Firth's drawing of Grandfather and me in Mrs. Bell's garden on a nail above my bed. Same bed, same house, but everything different.

My cousin Cora picked the night Aunt Tillie's house was to be moved to have her baby. It was a little boy that Grandmother, who was there for the birthing, said looked exactly like Raymond. They decided to name him Freedom, for the home he was leaving. And the next day Aunt Flora's daughter Grace announced that she and Lester had run off and got married and she was going with him to Topeka. So there was Aunt Flora in our kitchen, bawling just like Aunt Tillie did, and all of us weeping, too.

I had one more blow coming:

"Lewis Hembry's going," Poppa said. "They're moving on up to Oklahoma."

"But they can't!" I cried. First Bessie, and now Lou Ann, my two best friends.

"Can and will, baby," Poppa said. "Asked the railroad for a transfer, and they said they'll give it to him."

If we weren't busy moving houses, we were saying good-bye.

That same week the Ragsdales left, taking the album quilt Grandmother stitched together for them, and their house was moved out to The Flats and set down across the street from ours. Aunt Susannah set to work fixing it up. People who left gave her the furniture they didn't need or want to take along, and it got so you could go in her house and find a little bit of your old friends and neighbors. Aunt Susannah was about the only person there who seemed to be happy about something.

Finally it was Grandfather's turn to haul his house. It was about the only one left. But Grandmother was still insisting she wasn't going.

"We'll have to do the packing for her," Momma said wearily. "She's being as stubborn as I've ever seen her."

When the men came to move the house, Grandmother Lila refused to come out. "I'm traveling with my house," she said, and she sat down in her rocking chair in the parlor and took out her fancywork.

Momma tried to coax her out, so did Aunt Tillie and Aunt Vinnie and Aunt Flora, but it was no good. She wouldn't budge. Then Grandfather said, "Rose Lee, you go in and sit with her. If she won't come out, we'll just take the house with her in it, that's all."

And so I did as I was told, gladly, and sat in the company rocking chair in Grandmother's parlor while the house she had lived in all her married life moved slowly, slowly through the dark night. It was an odd thing to be inside looking out as the men hollered to each other, bringing the hindmost log up to the front, over and over and over again as we rolled toward The Flats.

"Grandmother," I said, to pass the time while Freedomtown was left behind, "tell me about when you met Grandfather." I was thinking of my trip with him from the fairgrounds on the Fourth of July, and Grandfather's story of his vision of a wife. I wondered if she knew about that.

Grandmother bit off a length of embroidery floss, threaded her needle, and plunged it through the cloth stretched tight on her hoop. "I had a number of young men calling on me," she said. The needle appeared from under the hoop and disappeared again. "Some were handsomer than Jim Williams, some earned plenty more money, but—" Her voice trailed off, and I saw she was smiling.

"But *what?*"

"He was just so *insistent,*" she said. "He kept saying 'I had a vision of you, Lila,' or some such foolishness, and somehow I believed him." She laughed to herself. "Next thing I knew, I was married."

"But how did you know he was the best one, Grandmother? Did you have a dream or anything?"

"No, but I had a feeling. Just a feeling he would be kind. And I was right. Believe it or not, the only thing we ever argued about is this business." She waved her hand to include the house, the men and mules outside, our slow progress toward The Flats.

By the time the sun came up, Grandfather's house stood solidly in its new place. Grandmother rose calmly from her rocking chair, tucked her wiry gray hair into its bun, and marched into her kitchen just like it was any ordinary morning. She built a fire in her cook-stove, found her iron skillet, and began frying up some bacon. She put the coffee on to boil and set a pan of biscuits on the stove to heat up.

When breakfast was ready, she called to Grandfather Jim. We sat down at the table, already covered with a snow white cloth embroidered with yellow daisies, and bowed our heads and gave thanks for the bounties that God had bestowed upon us.

Then I went off to school at the Knights of Pythias Hall, taking the long walk down Ragsdale Avenue.

Emily Dickinson

Because I could not stop for Death

Emily Dickinson offers an unusual vision of death.

Because I could not stop for Death—
He kindly stopped for me—
The Carriage held but just Ourselves—
And Immortality.

5 We slowly drove—He knew no haste
And I had put away
My labor and my leisure too,
For His Civility—

We passed the School, where Children strove
10 At Recess—in the Ring—
We passed the Fields of Gazing Grain—
We passed the Setting Sun—

Or rather—He passed Us—
The Dews drew quivering and chill—
15 For only Gossamer, my Gown—
My Tippet—only Tulle—

We paused before a House that seemed
A Swelling of the Ground—
The Roof was scarcely visible—
20   The Cornice—in the Ground—

Since then—'tis Centuries—and yet
Feels shorter than the Day
I first surmised the Horses' Heads
Were toward Eternity—

c. 1863

Edgar Lee Masters

Lucinda Matlock

In this poem, Lucinda looks back on her long life—
the good times as well as the bad.

I went to the dances at Chandlerville,
And played snap-out at Winchester.
One time we changed partners,
Driving home in the moonlight of middle June,
5   And then I found Davis.
We were married and lived together for seventy years,
Enjoying, working, raising the twelve children,
Eight of whom we lost
Ere I had reached the age of sixty.
10   I spun, I wove, I kept the house, I nursed the sick,
I made the garden, and for holiday
Rambled over the fields where sang the larks,
And by Spoon River gathering many a shell,
And many a flower and medicinal weed—
15   Shouting to the wooded hills, singing to the green valleys.
At ninety-six I had lived enough, that is all,
And passed to a sweet repose.
What is this I hear of sorrow and weariness,
Anger, discontent and drooping hopes?
20   Degenerate sons and daughters,
Life is too strong for you—
It takes life to love Life.

Sinclair Lewis

from
Main Street

In this excerpt from Sinclair Lewis's acclaimed novel about small-town life, Carol Kennicott has arrived from the city to begin her new life as the wife of a local physician.

WHEN CAROL HAD WALKED for thirty-two minutes she had completely covered the town, east and west, north and south; and she stood at the corner of Main Street and Washington Avenue and despaired.

Main Street with its two-story brick shops, its story-and-a-half wooden residences, its muddy expanse from concrete walk to walk, its huddle of Fords and lumber-wagons, was too small to absorb her. The broad, straight, unenticing gashes of the streets let in the grasping prairie on every side. She realized the vastness and the emptiness of the land. The skeleton iron windmill on the farm a few blocks away, at the north end of Main Street, was like the ribs of a dead cow. She thought of the coming of the Northern winter, when the unprotected houses would crouch together in terror of storms galloping out of that wild waste. They were so small and weak, the little brown houses. They were shelters for sparrows, not homes for warm laughing people.

She told herself that down the street the leaves were a splendor. The maples were orange; the oaks a solid tint of raspberry. And the lawns had been nursed with love. But the thought would not hold. At best the trees resembled a thinned woodlot. There was no park to rest the eyes. And since not Gopher Prairie but Wakamin was the county-seat, there was no courthouse with its grounds.

She glanced through the fly-specked windows of the most pretentious building in sight, the one place which welcomed strangers and determined their opinion of the charm and luxury of Gopher Prairie—the Minniemashie House. It was a tall lean shabby structure, three stories of yellow-streaked wood, the corners covered with sanded pine slabs purporting to symbolize stone. In the hotel office she could see a stretch of bare unclean floor, a line of rickety chairs with brass cuspidors between, a writing-desk with advertisements in mother-of-pearl letters upon the glass-covered back. The dining-room beyond was a jungle of stained table-cloths and catsup bottles.

She looked no more at the Minniemashie House.

A man in cuffless shirt-sleeves with pink arm-garters, wearing a linen collar but no tie, yawned his way from Dyer's Drug Store across to the hotel. He leaned against the wall, scratched a while, sighed, and in a bored way gossiped with a man tilted back in a chair. A lumber-wagon, its long green box filled with large spools of barbed-wire fencing, creaked down the block. A Ford, in reverse, sounded as though it were shaking to pieces, then recovered and rattled away. In the Greek candy-store was the whine of a peanut-roaster, and the oily smell of nuts.

There was no other sound nor sign of life.

She wanted to run, fleeing from the encroaching prairie, demanding the security of a great city. Her dreams of creating a beautiful town were ludicrous. Oozing out from every drab wall, she felt a forbidding spirit which she could never conquer.

She trailed down the street on one side, back on the other, glancing into the cross streets. It was a private Seeing Main Street tour. She was within ten minutes beholding not only the heart of a place called Gopher Prairie, but ten thousand towns from Albany to San Diego:

Dyer's Drug Store, a corner building of regular and unreal blocks of artificial stone. Inside the store, a greasy marble soda-fountain with an electric lamp of red and green and curdled-yellow mosaic shade. Pawed-over heaps of tooth-brushes and combs and packages of shaving-soap. Shelves of soap-cartons, teething-rings, garden-seeds, and patent medicines in yellow packages—nostrums for consumption, for "women's diseases"—notorious mixtures of opium and alcohol, in the very shop to which her husband sent patients for the filling of prescriptions.

From a second-story window the sign "W. P. Kennicott, Phys. & Surgeon," gilt on black sand.

A small wooden motion-picture theater called "The Rosebud Movie Palace." Lithographs announcing a film called "Fatty in Love."

Howland & Gould's Grocery. In the display window, black, overripe bananas and lettuce on which a cat was sleeping. Shelves lined with red crêpe paper which was now faded and torn and concentrically spotted. Flat against the wall of the second story the signs of lodges—the Knights of Pythias, the Maccabees, the Woodmen, the Masons.

Dahl & Oleson's Meat Market—a reek of blood.

A jewelry shop with tinny-looking wrist-watches for women. In front of it, at the curb, a huge wooden clock which did not go. . . .

A clothing store with a display of "ox-blood-shade Oxfords with bulldog toes." Suits which looked worn and glossless while they were still new, flabbily draped on dummies like corpses with painted cheeks.

The Bon Ton Store—Haydock & Simons'—the largest shop in town.

The first-story front of clear glass, the plates cleverly bound at the edges with brass. The second story of pleasant tapestry brick. One window of excellent clothes for men, interspersed with collars of floral pique which showed mauve daisies on a saffron ground. Newness and an obvious notion of neatness and service. Haydock & Simons. Haydock. She had met a Haydock at the station; Harry Haydock; an active person of thirty-five. He seemed great to her, now, and very like a saint. His shop was clean!

Axel Egge's General Store, frequented by Scandinavian farmers. In the shallow dark window-space heaps of sleazy sateens, badly woven galateas, canvas shoes designed for women with bulging ankles, steel and red glass buttons upon cards with broken edges, a cottony blanket, a granite-ware frying-pan reposing on a sun-faded crepe blouse.

Sam Clark's Hardware Store. An air of frankly metallic enterprise. Guns and churns and barrels of nails and beautiful shiny butcher knives.

Chester Dashaway's House Furnishing Emporium. A vista of heavy oak rockers with leather seats, asleep in a dismal row.

Billy's Lunch. Thick handleless cups on the wet oilcloth-covered counter. An odor of onions and the smoke of hot lard. In the doorway a young man audibly sucking a toothpick.

The warehouse of the buyer of cream and potatoes. The sour smell of a dairy.

The Ford Garage and the Buick Garage, competent one-story brick and cement buildings opposite each other. Old and new cars on grease-blackened concrete floors. Tire advertisements. The roaring of a tested motor; a racket which beat at the nerves. Surly young men in khaki union-overalls. The most energetic and vital places in town.

A large warehouse for agricultural implements. An impressive barricade of green and gold wheels, of shafts and sulky seats, belonging to machinery of which Carol knew nothing—potato-planters, manure-spreaders, silage-cutters, disk-harrows, breaking-plows.

A feed store, its windows opaque with the dust of bran, a patent medicine advertisement painted on its roof.

Ye Art Shoppe, Prop. Mrs. Mary Ellen Wilks, Christian Science Library open daily free. A touching fumble at beauty. A one-room shanty of boards recently covered with rough stucco. A show-window delicately rich in error: vases starting out to imitate tree-trunks but running off into blobs of gilt—an aluminum ash-tray labeled "Greetings from Gopher Prairie"—a Christian Science magazine—a stamped sofa-cushion portraying a large ribbon tied to a small poppy, the correct skeins of embroidery-silk lying on the pillow. Inside the shop, a glimpse of bad carbon prints of bad and famous pictures, shelves of phonograph records and camera films, wooden toys, and in the midst an anxious small woman sitting in a padded rocking chair.

A barber shop and pool room. A man in shirt sleeves, presumably Del Snafflin the proprietor, shaving a man who had a large Adam's apple.

Nat Hicks's Tailor Shop, on a side street off Main. A one-story building. A fashion-plate showing human pitchforks in garments which looked as hard as steel plate.

On another side street a raw red-brick Catholic Church with a varnished yellow door.

The post-office—merely a partition of glass and brass shutting off the rear of a mildewed room which must once have been a shop. A tilted writing-shelf against a wall rubbed black and scattered with official notices and army recruiting-posters.

The damp, yellow-brick schoolbuilding in its cindery grounds.

The State Bank, stucco masking wood.

The Farmers' National Bank. An Ionic temple of marble. Pure, exquisite, solitary. A brass plate with "Ezra Stowbody, Pres't."

A score of similar shops and establishments.

Behind them and mixed with them, the houses, meek cottages or large, comfortable, soundly uninteresting symbols of prosperity.

In all the town not one building save the Ionic bank which gave pleasure to Carol's eyes; not a dozen buildings which suggested that, in the fifty years of Gopher Prairie's existence, the citizens had realized that it was either desirable or possible to make this, their common home, amusing or attractive.

It was not only the unsparing unapologetic ugliness and the rigid straightness which overwhelmed her. It was the planlessness, the flimsy temporariness of the buildings, their faded unpleasant colors. The street was cluttered with electric-light poles, telephone poles, gasoline pumps for motor cars, boxes of goods. Each man had built with the most valiant disregard of all the others. Between a large new "block" of two-story brick shops on one side, and the fire-brick Overland garage on the other side, was a one-story cottage turned into a millinery shop. The white temple of the Farmers' Bank was elbowed back by a grocery of glaring yellow brick. One store-building had a patchy galvanized iron cornice; the building beside it was crowned with battlements and pyramids of brick capped with blocks of red sandstone.

She escaped from Main Street, fled home.

She wouldn't have cared, she insisted, if the people had been comely. She had noted a young man loafing before a shop, one unwashed hand holding the cord of an awning; a middle-aged man who had a way of staring at women as though he had been married too long and too prosaically; an old farmer, solid, wholesome, but not clean—his face like a potato fresh from the earth. None of them had shaved for three days.

"If they can't build shrines, out here on the prairie, surely there's nothing to prevent their buying safety-razors!" she raged.

She fought herself: "I must be wrong. People do live here. It *can't* be as ugly as—as I know it is! I must be wrong. But I can't do it. I can't go through with it."

She came home too seriously worried for hysteria; and when she found Kennicott waiting for her, and exulting, "Have a walk? Well, like the town? Great lawns and trees, eh?" she was able to say, with a self-protective maturity new to her, "It's very interesting."

III

The train which brought Carol to Gopher Prairie also brought Miss Bea Sorenson.

Miss Bea was a stalwart, corn-colored, laughing young woman, and she was bored by farm-work. She desired the excitements of city-life, and the way to enjoy city-life was, she had decided, to "go get a yob as hired girl in Gopher Prairie." She contentedly lugged her pasteboard telescope from the station to her cousin, Tina Malmquist, maid of all work in the residence of Mrs. Luke Dawson.

"Vell, so you come to town," said Tina.

"Ya. Ay get a yob," said Bea.

"Vell. . . . You got a fella now?"

"Ya. Yim Yacobson."

"Vell. I'm glat to see you. How much you vant a veek?"

"Sex dollar."

"There ain't nobody pay dat. Vait! Dr. Kennicott, I t'ink he marry a girl from de Cities. Maybe she pay dat. Vell. You go take a valk."

"Ya," said Bea.

So it chanced that Carol Kennicott and Bea Sorenson were viewing Main Street at the same time.

Bea had never before been in a town larger than Scandia Crossing, which has sixty-seven inhabitants.

As she marched up the street she was meditating that it didn't hardly seem like it was possible there could be so many folks all in one place at the same time. My! It would take years to get acquainted with them all. And swell people, too! A fine big gentleman in a new pink shirt with a diamond, and not no washed-out blue denim working-shirt. A lovely lady in a longery dress (but it must be an awful hard dress to wash). And the stores!

Not just three of them, like there were at Scandia Crossing, but more than four whole blocks!

The Bon Ton Store—big as four barns—my! it would simply scare a person to go in there, with seven or eight clerks all looking at you. And the men's suits, on figures just like human. And Axel Egge's, like home, lots of Swedes and Norskes in there, and a card of dandy buttons, like rubies.

A drug store with a soda fountain that was just huge, awful long, and all lovely marble; and on it there was a great big lamp with the biggest shade you ever saw—all different kinds colored glass stuck together; and the soda spouts, they were silver, and they came right out of the bottom of the lamp-stand! Behind the fountain there were glass shelves, and bottles of new kinds of soft drinks, that nobody ever heard of. Suppose a fella took you *there!*

A hotel, awful high, higher than Oscar Tollefson's new red barn; three stories, one right on top of another; you had to stick your head back to look clear up to the top. There was a swell traveling man in there—probably been to Chicago, lots of times.

Oh, the dandiest people to know here! There was a lady going by, you wouldn't hardly say she was any older than Bea herself; she wore a dandy new gray suit and black pumps. She almost looked like she was looking over the town, too. But you couldn't tell what she thought. Bea would like to be that way—kind of quiet, so nobody would get fresh. Kind of—oh, elegant.

A Lutheran Church. Here in the city there'd be lovely sermons, and church twice on Sunday, *every* Sunday!

And a movie show!

A regular theater, just for movies. With the sign "Change of bill every evening." Pictures every evening!

There were movies in Scandia Crossing, but only once every two weeks, and it took the Sorensons an hour to drive in—papa was such a tightwad he wouldn't get a Ford. But here she could put on her hat any evening, and in three minutes' walk be to the movies, and see lovely fellows in dress-suits and Bill Hart and everything!

How could they have so many stores? Why! There was one just for to-bacco alone, and one (a lovely one—the Art Shoppy it was) for pictures and vases and stuff, with oh, the dandiest vase made so it looked just like a tree trunk!

Bea stood on the corner of Main Street and Washington Avenue. The roar of the city began to frighten her. There were five automobuls on the street all at the same time—and one of 'em was a great big car that must of cost two thousand dollars—and the 'bus was starting for a train with five elegant-dressed fellows, and a man was pasting up red bills with lovely pictures of washing-machines on them, and the jeweler was laying out bracelets and wrist-watches and *everything* on real velvet.

What did she care if she got six dollars a week? Or two! It was worth while working for nothing, to be allowed to stay here. And think how it would be in the evening, all lighted up—and not with no lamps, but with electrics! And maybe a gentleman friend taking you to the movies and buying you a strawberry ice cream soda!

Bea trudged back.

Brooks Atkinson | # The Play

In this review from the New York Times, *theater critic Brooks Atkinson praises the Broadway opening of* Our Town *on February 4, 1938.*

ALTHOUGH THORNTON WILDER is celebrated chiefly for his fiction, it will be necessary now to reckon with him as a dramatist. His "Our Town," which opened at Henry Miller's last evening, is a beautifully evocative play. Taking as his material three periods in the history of a placid New Hampshire town, Mr. Wilder has transmuted the simple events of human life into universal reverie. He has given familiar facts a deeply moving, philosophical perspective. Staged without scenery and with the curtain always up, "Our Town" has escaped from the formal barrier of the modern theatre into the quintessence of acting, thought and speculation. In the staging, Jed Harris has appreciated the rare quality of Mr. Wilder's handiwork and illuminated it with a shining performance. "Our Town" is, in this column's opinion, one of the finest achievements of the current stage.

* * *

Since the form is strange, this review must attempt to explain the purpose of the play. It is as though Mr. Wilder were saying: "Now for evidence as to the way Americans were living in the early part of the century, take Grover Corners, N.H., as an average town. Mark it 'Exhibit A' in American folkways." His spokesman in New Hampshire cosmology is Frank Craven, the best pipe and pants-pocket actor in the business, who experimentally sets the stage with tables and chairs before the house lights go down and then prefaces the performance with a few general remarks about Grover Corners. Under his benign guidance we see three periods in career of one generation of Grover Corners folks—"Life," "Love" and "Death."

* * *

Literally, they are not important. On one side of an imaginary street Dr. Gibbs and his family are attending to their humdrum affairs with relish and probity. On the opposite side Mr. Webb, the local editor, and his family are fulfilling their quiet destiny. Dr. Gibbs's boy falls in love with Mr. Webb's girl—neighbors since birth. They marry after graduating from high school;

she dies several years later in childbirth and she is buried on Cemetery Hill. Nothing happens in the play that is not normal and natural and ordinary.

* * *

But by stripping the play of everything that is not essential, Mr. Wilder has given it a profound, strange, unworldly significance. This is less the portrait of a town than the sublimation of the commonplace; and in contrast with the universe that silently swims around it, it is brimming over with compassion. Most of it is a tender idyll in the kindly economy of Mr. Wilder's literary style; some of it is heartbreaking in the mute simplicity of human tragedy. For in the last act, which is entitled "Death," Mr. Wilder shows the dead of Grover Corners sitting peacefully in their graves and receiving into their quiet company a neighbor's girl whom they love. So Mr. Wilder's pathetically humble evidence of human living passes into the wise beyond. Grover Corners is a green corner of the universe.

* * *

With about the best script of his career in his hands, Mr. Harris has risen nobly to the occasion. He has reduced theatre to its lowest common denominator without resort to perverse showmanship. As chorus, preacher, drug store proprietor and finally as shepherd of the flock, Frank Craven plays with great sincerity and understanding, keeping the sublime well inside his homespun style. As the boy and girl, John Craven, who is Frank Craven's son, and Martha Scott turn youth into tremulous idealization, some of their scenes are lovely past all enduring. Jay Fassett as Dr. Gibbs, Evelyn Varden as his wife, Thomas W. Ross and Helen Carew as the Webbs play with an honesty that is enriching. There are many other good bits of acting.

* * *

Out of respect for the detached tone of Mr. Wilder's script the performance as a whole is subdued and understated. The scale is so large that the voices are never lifted. But under the leisurely monotone of the production there is a fragment of the immortal truth. "Our Town" is a microcosm. It is also a hauntingly beautiful play.

Olivia Castellano

Prologue for *The Comstock Journals* (or *Sotol City Blues*)

Many people form a strong bond with their hometowns. Hometowns are places where important lessons are first learned, identities are shaped, and life can seem both simple and magical.

A FEW YEARS BACK, if anyone had told me you could find comfort in the memory of a town, I would have thought them insane. If they had said that on the brink of madness what can keep you from falling over the edge would be the memory of a town and a girl who believed in magic—I would not have believed them.

But through the years, this is what has happened to me with Comstock, an insignificant southwest Tex-Mex border town where I lived as a girl, trapped between earth and sky for what seemed an eternity. To escape, I invented a blue garden and horse with enormous wings. Comstock was already an old woman about to die. Yet, because she knew I was a dreamer, she held me in her arms away from hurt and let me dream in a time when everything was uncertain and dreams were all you could ever be sure of.

It is vanity to think your childhood town special. But what you take from a place you must in some way give back. Because in its final hour, a town gathers itself in and reclaims its own, or at least those who remained faithful in spirit. It pulls back everything it once gave life to. A town remembers everything. And in the final analysis, when you have to settle accounts, you must pay back.

I have not tried to hold on to Comstock; it has held on to me. In my deepest delirium the voices I heard were the same ones I heard in Grandpa's garden and the song they sang was his favorite: "En el cielo, en la tierra, en el mar; en la tumba estaremos los dos."*

Whenever I close my eyes, I see a girl and an old man walking hand in hand in early evening, a bright orange moon behind them. They are crossing a wide open plain—yellow dust on their bare feet and the wind in their hair. For a second, they are happy. Then they turn to see their mad pursuers—a madman with ropes around his waist, brujas laughing and wearing white chiffon dresses, women with butcher knives high in the air ready to strike—and the girl and the old man break into a run. This image comes in dreams or when the night is quiet.

Grandpa Francisco Ruelas Guerrero lies buried in the cemetery just beyond the last railroad crossing between Comstock and Del Rio. Uncle Manuel of the Ropes died a model patient in a mental hospital in San Antonio; the brujas too are dead, and the aunts of the butcher knives take pills to control the urge to kill. I have tried in small ways to appease their ghosts, have written poems to them and sang them songs. But this has not been enough.

I have been more faithful to Comstock than I planned. She let me live each day believing life was good and God was everywhere in her yellow, bleak terrain. Because of her, the earth was magic and the sky for dreamers. She lived in all of us, but only I believed in her. It is only natural she chose me to dream her into today.

Whenever things got too sad or complex for my eight-year-old heart, I would stand in front of our house and look in all directions. I would hook my eyes at the horizon and sink into the small ocean of earth and sky that was Comstock. At a young age, I learned to define myself by becoming the space I inhabited. I willed myself into her landscape, defining myself by the Rio Grande to the south, la barranca and Devil's River to the northeast, and the Pecos to the west.

As I grew, I realized the world was a larger place, and limitless in terms of the spaces we could become. Soon, Comstock was not enough. To escape I invented a winged horse, blue horse of dreams, that I could ride high above south Texas to see what else I could be. The horse became a necessary dream. I didn't know then that it was all deception because there is no escape from that first country we shape as children, first enchantment with earth and sky, which we carry with us and touches everything we are to do and become.

---

*In the sky, on the earth, in the sea; in the grave the two of us will be together.

Someone once said that in memory everything happens to music. Comstock has become a singular song. In the face of memory, the heart and mind become a willing theatre. This is when you come to accept fully that a town lives on inside you. You look down from a lighting booth onto a huge bare stage washed in blue light. Slowly, you hear dogs barking, a girl singing a sad refrain ("En el cielo, en la tierra, en el mar . . ."). And they begin arriving. First, Grandpa Francisco and Odilia—he is an old man, gray hair and mustache; brown skin and high Tarascan cheekbones. He wears blue coveralls, steel-toe work boots, and a dirty hat. And she a thin girl of eight, her face bright, eyes large and inquisitive; hair in braids and her dress, blue gingham plaid with a large white collar and a bow tied in back. Then comes her mother, Remedios, the simple, soft-spoken woman, slender and dark with eyes like the girl's. Next, Uncle Manuel, hair standing on end as if some monstrosity keeps him perpetually frightened, his eyes wide and penetrating. Wearing khaki pants and shirt, he walks nervously as if many voices are calling from all directions. Others follow—aunts, uncles, brothers, sisters, fathers, niños, viejitos—toda la gente de Comstock. They arrive bewildered and dusty, having trekked across the wide yellow desert of memory and onto the stage of praise, hoping to be perfected in remembrance. The year is 1955; Odilia Magallanes is eight years old again. This is how I see them— again and again. Their memory follows me everywhere.

I don't pretend to know when my love affair with Comstock began, but whatever I feel for this town has everything to do with Francisco Ruelas Guerrero, my mother's father. Because of him, a blue horse flew across the early sky of my childhood imagination, and a world of ancient voices sang to me in his garden of blue light. For a child of eight discovering the world, he had just the right magic. It is healthy for a child to have heroes, but I worshipped him and knew enough about him on which to build a dream. Through the years and the slow unravelling of painful truths, I have come to see him as a man. But truth has not destroyed him in the heart where memories live. As I said, I was a hopeless dreamer, and Grandpa believed in dreams.

Later, in my grown-up bouts with madness, I came to doubt every nook and cranny of my existence. At times, I have even doubted whether Grandpa and Comstock ever existed. This is why I must tell their story—to confirm once and for all that they did exist. The grandfather I knew as a child was as real as the one I later discovered—who tried to kill his wife for her infidelities.

But, when you have held on to memory for so long, no new revelation must be allowed to change certain facts. Grandpa taught me to fly with my eyes and listen to voices. As long as I had faith, he said, I would be able to fly. In summer, he taught me to pray to the hot desert sand in the name of the Apache and Comanche blood spilled on those plains. These are facts a child holds on to. He showed me how to search for ominous red lights that hid among the chaparrales at night. He said they were the evil of money which Spaniards had taken away from the Indians and hidden, money and gold burning in their own red hell. And wherever a light landed, a buried treasure was to be found. Yet, one time he and a friend dug where a light had signalled. All night they dug, about seven feet deep, but all they found was a crate full of worms. Grandpa said his friend's jealousy had turned the treasure into evil.

And at night, he taught me to scan the sky for omens, falling stars and flashing lights—signs of birth and death, he'd say. Every time Grandpa saw a strange light in the sky, a child was born or someone died. Grandpa and Comstock had a secret link. So, whatever life Comstock had translated itself to me through him. He had become Comstock. Town and old man were one. As a child I knew this; as an adult, it took years to understand and accept. Children have a way of knowing things in their blood. And, if you are lucky, one day that special knowledge finds you—the words come to lie down on your skin or whisper in your ear. It took a long time for the words to find me.

It happened on the brink of insanity, in the delirium of self-destruction. Years of running away from myself, rebelling against everything I had become had led me into the black hole of a total breakdown out of which I almost didn't crawl. I had subconsciously tried to kill the child I had been. The brown, dusty Mexican girl who grew up in a racist southern town had come to hate what she had become. She tried to deny that she came from a long line of Mexican peasants and illiterates, that she had been spat on and called "dirty Meskin" so many times she knew the curl of a racist's lips just before the words were mouthed.

To compensate for self-hate, I had become obsessed with playing girl-wonder and trying to be all things to everyone else except myself. These acts of self-deception and self-hatred had led me to an insane nightmare-filled depression accompanied by a hopeless case of self-pity, total physical fatigue, and hallucinations. All I know is that one morning, at age twenty-six, I woke up unable to get out of bed or make sense of the world around me. I remained this way for one year. My parents refused to hospitalize me. I am sure if they had, diagnosis would have been borderline schizophrenia, which, once inside, would have blossomed into classic paranoia. Thank God, mine have always been a hardy people who took care of their own locos and misfits.

I, who had made promises to Grandpa that I would someday be a teacher and a poet, was now rotting in a bed, unable to make a simple phone call without falling apart or hold down a clerical job, though a master's degree in literature hung on my wall. I would go to sleep at night praying death would find me before morning; during the day, I would gaze into space, trying to erase myself.

One morning, about three or four months into the madness, I looked at the clock and realized its hands and numbers were incomprehensible and meaningless. "What time is it?" I asked my sister. "It is eleven in the morning," she said. But I had no notion what that meant. Time—like my life—had become irrelevant and illogical. Soon, in similar fashion, the names of days and months lost meaning. I could not even recall their names, much less list them in order. The boundaries of conventional reality were quickly giving way. Food and liquid inevitably landed on my chest as I lost track of the borders of my own body, of where space ended and my body began. I had started to fuse into emptiness.

A few weeks later, the whispering began. Such incredible whispering—like many voices of people on a telephone all talking at once or like a powerful recitation delivered in stage whispers by a huge chorus; at other times, it was more muffled, like when you put your ear to the locked door of a room where many people are conspiring against you.

One singular thought hit me: once I allowed myself to understand the voices, there would be no salvation. They would begin controlling, would command me to cross to the other side from which—once I crossed over—there would be no return. One day, I clearly made out the phrases, ". . . because you know she said . . ." and, "let me tell you about her . . ." A growing fear gripped me: they were talking about me! I felt persecuted by gossip-mongers who were spreading horrible gossip about me. Hallucinations of being dismembered by these voices and my bones left to rot on an open field began to haunt me. But, strangely enough, they also angered me. And thanks to my anger, I began a conscious effort to fight back. Whenever I sensed the voices coming, which usually began with a buzzing in the right ear which hit at any time, in broad daylight or in the deep dark night, I would drag myself to the bathroom or kitchen sink and splash cold water on my face, shaking my head from side to side as violently as my limited strength allowed. In the beginning, this would keep the whispering at bay. But, soon, the voices came more often and the whispering intensified. I could no longer make them stop.

"Dear God," I said to myself, "do I really hate myself this much? Is this how I want to end up—sitting in some mental ward talking to myself? Or worse, doing terrible things to others or myself at the command of some voice or devil of my own making?" With the voices came faces. Of this, I was certain. I had visions of becoming like my poor Uncle Manuel in Comstock, who, about an hour before an epileptic seizure hit him, would become a raving maniac; he'd talk to imaginary people, complain that faces were laughing at him and look for something or someone to destroy.

Strange. Now that death wearing the mask of insanity was knocking at my door, I wanted more than ever to live. I, who had hated myself, my past, my peasant origins, wanted to live. But, since everything inside me had already been erased—sense of self, love of family, sense of history and time—nothing was left to pry me from the grip of this madness. It became clear to me that to fight these voices and win, I would have to reinvent myself, to go far back to the waters of childhood.

The first chance available, I called my mother and my sister together and pleaded, "Please, tell me everything you can remember about Comstock." At first they tried to humor me by bringing up little incidents—how we picked wild strawberries (pitayas) en el monte behind the old schoolhouse and would get home looking like payasas, our faces smeared with the purple juice. Or how we'd go for long walks along the railroad tracks and stop to steal El Pollito's roses. He was an elderly man with white hair who lived alone by the railroad crossing and was thin and frail like a fragile little chicken—when he'd finally see us scurrying around his yard cutting flowers, he'd say, "Ustaydes, mushashas, qweren aqua?" We'd run, carrying the flowers in the lifted skirts of our dresses.

Soon talk shifted on to Grandpa Francisco, how happy we felt whenever he gazed upon us, how important and whole in his eyes. The more they reminisced, the more that Comstock began to sift into me with its yellow, dusty plains and blue open-armed sky—all began to shift and rearrange itself, slowly and crudely at first, like a collage of pictures drawn by very young children.

With all their generosity of spirit, my mother and sister—in the tradition of good raconteurs—began to weave a blanket of remembrance. And then, literally, as I gained strength, my sister Viviane would wrap a blanket around me and take me for long drives in the country. I would stare at the Sacramento River and its trees, begging them to come inside me. I needed to learn to see and feel again; but everything flitted by fast or in slow motion—trees, cars, houses—all exaggerated.

In the following weeks, the more they talked of Comstock, the more its yellow earth and blue horizon sifted into memory's eye. And as my past cleared, so did the present. Memories of earlier trees made these new trees more meaningful. Whenever I sensed the whispering coming, I would will myself into memories of Comstock, splashing them quickly on the disoriented canvas in my mind, using the palette of incidents my mother and sister were providing. "Comstock, where are you? Please help me!" I'd say whenever I heard a trace of whispering building up inside. With my eyes shut tight, I would pray with every cell in my body, every imagined ridge in my brain. And, sure enough, Comstock would come keening—its yellows and blues pounding on my eyelids. Being able to will myself into time past made me less fearful of the present. Also, the montage of past images somehow interfered with the whispering, reduced it to a mournful humming or a simple ringing in the ear. This continued for a long time, a battle of voices: the one of memory and the other of God knows what demons which were trying to build their house in my head.

Finally, one morning toward the end of this one-year journey into self-effacement I went to wash my face, and as I bent down over the bathroom sink I heard for the first time the voice of memory: a gentle feeling crawled up the back of my legs from the soles of my feet, and I felt a warm breath on my shoulders, as if someone were standing directly behind me. Then, I clearly recognized my grandfather's voice. "Hija," it said, "your time has not come. Do as you must before you lie down to rest." His soothing words, like small, warm hands, were lightly pressing on my upper arms. So palpably real was his presence that when I looked into the mirror, I expected to see Grandpa standing behind me though he had been dead twenty years. Alas, I was alone. Yet, for the first time in a year, I felt the corners of my mouth curling up in a smile. And, for the first time, I willed my own tears. I cried because a girl was standing in an open field, calling my name, "Odilia! Odilia!" Gently, she was calling, and an old man was coming to lead her by the hand. The two were walking home together once again. I stood like that for what seemed an eternity—peaceful, wonderful eternity—reliving entire scenes of the childhood I had spent with my grandfather. When I opened my eyes, Mother was knocking at the bathroom door, calling my name, asking if I was all right.

I knew at that moment that memory can sneak up and rescue us when we least expect it, and if we're lucky, we'll be ready when she comes. For the first time, I accepted that we are what we have been; to run away from that truth is to drive the self insane.

At year's end, I began a frenzied effort to recollect everything I could about Grandpa and Comstock. It was hopeless, because I was trying to remember as a little girl would recall her childhood town, much as I had done with my mother and sister's help. That particular Comstock had died for me long ago. What I really needed to recall was the Comstock that through the years had become Grandpa Francisco, the town layered with my own life.

It's the same as when you love someone through many years of joy and pain. Whenever you gaze at that person's face, it is no longer just one face but the layers of faces you have known and loved in that one person through the years. You see, Comstock is not just a town where I, Odilia Magallanes, lived as a girl and knew an old man who loved me beyond myself. It is many towns, the layers of memory itself, of the years that passed me while I held on to, destroyed, and rediscovered a girl, an old man, and an old woman named Comstock. It is layered with the knowledge that, in the face of time, memory and madness are at constant war. Do you see why I don't really know when this love affair began? We suffuse things we love with the essence of ourselves so that they no longer have a life of their own. In many ways, I have become Comstock; it has no life other than the one I give it. Too much has happened between us for someone else to tell her story. It is all vanity, a hopeless lover's possessiveness of a hopelessly unreal beloved.

Do you see, then, why I tread gently as I go back to my pathetic little group of peasants and illiterates whom I have learned to love? I must show them as they were before and after Time, the incredible magus with all the aces up his sleeve, tried to destroy them for me; and before Love, master of deception, distorted them in the deepest heart of memory. I must show them as insanity tried to use their voices against me.

I want to say simply that they lived, through everything—poor unedu-cated "Meskins," my people—heroic, brown, tragic and beautiful; they lived with hope because to have given up would have been against God, against life. They lived with all the humility they could muster in their collective ignorance. Now, in all their violence and sorrow, they live on, tied right here to me. I need to say, finally, this is where it all began, and I can put it all to rest. These are the sandy plains where a girl could draw strength from the mesquites and chaparral.

Comstock, when I lived there as a child, was a dreary, lonely place where one could get close to nature's mystery. The wind moaned and dust devils danced around us. It is about fifteen miles from the Rio Grande to the south, and about the same distance from the Pecos River on the west. Devil's River is to the northeast. The ground was both blessed and cursed long before my clan crossed its horizon. We lived so isolated that to survive we befriended the howling wind and yellow earth. Originally, its name was Sotol City, named for the sotol plant that grew in huge clusters everywhere. A piece of land nestled by three rivers had its own enchantment. But for me, it was Grandpa who made it fertile in the heart. In my earliest recollections, he was always there. And, whenever he gazed upon me or laid a gentle hand upon my head, the open plains and clear blue sky were one.

When the power of the earth reaches you through the love of a pure-spirited old man, you are twice blessed. Sometimes, however, I think the town and the old man knew all this would come to pass—that I would be-come obsessed with their memory, that they invented me, and dreamed me into the future simply to tell their story. I have no other life I can call my own. Conspiracy of memory and madness—Comstock, Grandpa, and I handcuffed through eternity. Toda mi gente de Comstock lie buried in the old cemetery next to the last railroad crossing on the road to Del Rio. All chose to be buried in the bowels of Comstock as if to say, "You made sure life would not defeat us, time would not forget us; now we offer ourselves to you."

Once I tell their story, everything can settle down and come to rest, undisturbed through the yellow sands of time, until someday, somewhere, a child not yet born will grow to tell the story of another town, another magical old man. To have this hope is to know finally in your heart that God exists. We can say, "Oh, let me tell you this or that story." But what we really mean is, "Let me tell you how I came to learn God lives, how a town and an old man taught me to love and give life, to bring out the dead and let them breathe again."

Acknowledgments *Continued from page ii*

Our Town. Copyright © 1938, 1965 by Thornton Wilder. All rights reserved. Printed in the United States of America. No part of this book may be used or reproduced in any manner whatsoever without written permission except in the case of brief quotations embodied in critical articles and reviews. For information address HarperCollins Publishers, Inc., 10 East 53rd Street, New York, NY 10022.

HarperCollins books may be purchased for educational, business, or sales promotional use. For information please write: Special Markets Department, HarperCollins Publishers, Inc., 10 East 53rd Street, New York, NY 10022.

Cover Art: *Adam's House*, 1928, Edward Hopper. Francis G. Mayer/CORBIS.